R. Gupta's®

Delhi
GENERAL KNOWLEDGE

A Complete Description of History, Geography, Economy, Polity, Flora & Fauna, Culture and more ...

2020
EDITION

Ramesh Publishing House, New Delhi

Published by
O.P. Gupta *for* Ramesh Publishing House

Admin. Office
12-H, New Daryaganj Road, Opp. Officers' Mess,
New Delhi-110002 ✆ 23261567, 23275224, 23275124

E-mail: info@rameshpublishinghouse.com
Website: www.rameshpublishinghouse.com

Showroom
● Balaji Market, Nai Sarak, Delhi-6 ✆ 23253720, 23282525
● 4457, Nai Sarak, Delhi-6, ✆ 23918938

Book Code: R-464
ISBN: 978-81-942336-5-7
HSN Code: 49011010

Contents

••••••

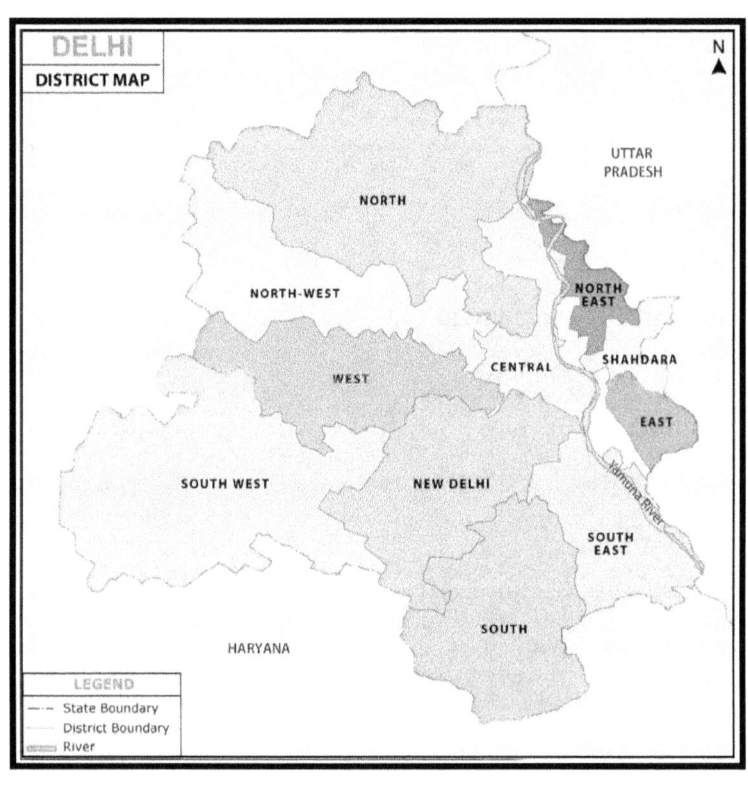

DELHI
DISTRICT MAP
N
UTTAR PRADESH
NORTH
NORTH-WEST
NORTH EAST
SHAHDARA
WEST
CENTRAL
EAST
SOUTH WEST
NEW DELHI
Yamuna River
SOUTH EAST
HARYANA
SOUTH
LEGEND
State Boundary
District Boundary
River

Who's Who

STATE GOVERNMENT

Lieutenant Governor
Anil Baijal

Chief Minister
Arvind Kejriwal

Arvind Kejriwal

❖	**Arvind Kejriwal**	Chief Minister, Water
❖	**Manish Sisodia**	Deputy Chief Minister/Education, Finance, Planning, Land & Building, Vigilance Services, Women and Child, Tourism, Art, Culture and Languages. All other departments not specifically allotted to any Minister.
❖	**Gopal Rai**	Employment, Development, Labour, General Administration Department, Irrigation and Flood Control.
❖	**Satyendar Jain**	Health, Industries, Public Works Department, Power, Home, Urban Development.
❖	**Kailash Gahlot**	Administrative Reforms, Information & Technology, Law, Justice & Legislative Affairs, Revenue, Transport, Environment and Forest.
❖	**Imran Hussain**	Food & Supply, Election.
❖	**Rajendra Pal Gautam**	Gurdwara Elections, SC & ST, Social Welfare, Cooperative.

MEMBERS OF LEGISLATIVE ASSEMBLY

Assembly Election–2015

Sr.no.	Members Name	Political Party	Constituency Name
1.	Pawan Kumar Sharma	AAP	Adarsh Nagar
2.	Ajay Dutt	AAP	Ambedkar Nagar
3.	Gopal Rai	AAP	Babarpur
4.	Narayan Dutt Sharma	AAP	Badarpur
5.	Ajesh Yadav	AAP	Badli
6.	Imran Hussain	AAP	Ballimaran
7.	Ram Chander	AAP	Bawana
8.	Col. Devinder Sehrawat	AAP	Bijwasan
9.	Sanjeev Jha	AAP	Burari
10.	Alka Lamba	AAP	Chandni Chowk
11.	Kartar Singh Tanwar	AAP	Chhatarpur
12.	Surender Singh	AAP	Delhi Cantonment
13.	Prakash	AAP	Deoli
14.	Adarsh Shastri	AAP	Dwarka
15.	Anil Kumar Bajpai	AAP	Gandhi Nagar
16.	Shri Dutt Sharma	AAP	Ghonda
17.	Fateh Singh	AAP	Gokalpur
18.	Saurabh Bharadwaj	AAP	Greater Kailash
19.	Jagdeep Singh	AAP	Hari Nagar
20.	Rajesh Rishi	AAP	Janakpuri
21.	Praveen Kumar	AAP	Jangpura
22.	Avtar Singh	AAP	Kalkaji
23.	Kapil Mishra	AAP	Karawal Nagar
24.	Vishesh Ravi	AAP	Karol Bagh
25.	Madan Lal	AAP	Kasturba Nagar
26.	Rituraj Govind	AAP	Kirari
27.	Manoj Kumar	AAP	Kondli
28.	S.K. Bagga	AAP	Krishna Nagar
29.	Nitin Tyagi	AAP	Laxmi Nagar
30.	Girish Soni	AAP	Madipur
31.	Somnath Bharti	AAP	Malviya Nagar
32.	Rakhi Birla	AAP	Mangol Puri
33.	Asim Ahmed Khan	AAP	Matia Mahal

Sr.no.	Members Name	Political Party	Constituency Name
34.	Gulab Singh	AAP	Matiala
35.	Naresh Yadav	AAP	Mehrauli
36.	Akhilesh Pati Tripathi	AAP	Model Town
37.	Shiv Charan Goel	AAP	Moti Nagar
38.	Sukhvir Singh	AAP	Mundka
39.	Jagdish Pradhan	BJP	Mustafabad
40.	Kailash Gahlot	AAP	Najafgarh
41.	Raghuvinder Shokeen	AAP	Nangloi Jat
42.	Sharad Kumar	AAP	Narela
43.	Arvind Kejriwal	AAP	New Delhi
44.	Amanatullah Khan	AAP	Okhla
45.	Bhavna Gaur	AAP	Palam
46.	Hazari Lal Chauhan	AAP	Patel Nagar
47.	Manish Sisodia	AAP	Patparganj
48.	Parmila Tokas	AAP	R.K. Puram
49.	Vijender Garg Vijay	AAP	Rajinder Nagar
50.	Manjinder Singh Sirsa	BJP	Rajouri Garden
51.	Mohinder Goyal	AAP	Rithala
52.	Vijender Kumar	BJP	Rohini
53.	Sarita Singh	AAP	Rohtas Nagar
54.	Som Dutt	AAP	Sadar Bazar
55.	Dinesh Mohaniya	AAP	Sangam Vihar
56.	Mohd. Ishraque	AAP	Seelampur
57.	Rajendra Pal Gautam	AAP	Seema Puri
58.	Ram Niwas Goel	AAP	Shahdara
59.	Satyendar Jain	AAP	Shakur Basti
60.	Bandana Kumari	AAP	Shalimar Bagh
61.	Sandeep Kumar	AAP	Sultanpur Majra
62.	Jarnail Singh	AAP	Tilak Nagar
63.	Pankaj Pushkar	AAP	Timarpur
64.	Jitender Singh Tomar	AAP	Tri Nagar
65.	Raju Dhingan	AAP	Trilokpuri
66.	Sahi Ram	AAP	Tughlakabad
67.	Naresh Balyan	AAP	Uttam Nagar
68.	Mahinder Yadav	AAP	Vikaspuri
69.	Om Prakash Sharma	BJP	Vishwas Nagar
70.	Rajesh Gupta	AAP	Wazirpur

Current Affairs

BUDGET 2019-20

The Delhi Deputy Chief Minister and Finance Minister Manish Sisodia on February 26, 2019 presented a ₹ 60,000 crore Budget for 2019-20 laying emphasis on education, health and transport sectors and said it is two times more than the one presented in 2014-15. Allocation for entrepreneurship plans, introduction of family business curriculum, setting up of a teachers training university and an applied science university are among the various initiatives announced in the Budget. The deputy chief minister said the free wi-fi project of the Aam Aadmi Party (AAP) government would start in the next financial year. Under the doorstep delivery programmes, 100 services would be brought under it, Sisodia said adding that ₹ 500 crore has been allocated in the budget for the CCTV project. There has been an increase of 73 per cent in the Budget for infrastructure projects and in transport sector, Mr Sisodia said adding that 4,000 new buses are being procured by the government which would materialise by the next financial year. The deputy CM said ₹ 100 crore has been allocated for a state electric vehicle fund. An amount of ₹ 7,485 has been allocated for the health sector, he said adding that a new scheme will also be launched to provide financial help to differently abled parents for marriage of their daughters. Mr Sisodia said ₹ 600 crore has been allocated for development work in unauthorised colonies while the total outlay for the transport sector has been kept at ₹ 1,807 crore, which is twice than the last fiscal. The AAP government allocated over ₹ 15,000 crore to education sector for 2019-20. The allocation to education is around 26 per cent of the total Budget.

INDIA'S NATIONAL WAR MEMORIAL

Nearly six decades after it was first proposed, Prime Minister Narendra Modi on February 25, 2019 inaugurated the National War Memorial, sprawled over 40 acres at the India Gate complex in the heart of the national capital. The Memorial has five concentric circles, named **Rakshak Chakra, Amar Chakra, Veerta Chakra, Tyag Chakra, Param Yodha Sthal** a central stone obelisk, and an eternal flame. The centre of the complex lies at a lower level than the surrounding features. The Memorial has been built at a cost of ₹ 176 crore.

Delhi
GENERAL KNOWLEDGE

Introduction 1

DELHI's significance lies in its traditional and historical status. This is a city— state now. Delhi has been the capital of India for thousands of years. It has, perhaps, seen more of history than any other city in India. Only a few cities in the world can compete with it as the capital of a great country for so many centuries. It has been a separate Union Territory ever since India became a free nation. After many debates and trials it was given limited autonomy in 1993, when the National Capital Region of Delhi was created with a kind of diarchy.

There was a time when Delhi was important only as a centre of historical monuments and known as a government city full of bureaucrats. But Delhi had always been a major business centre. In recent years, it has developed as a metropolis. That is important not only because it is not only the seat of the central government, but also it is a place where people live and experience the joy of living in a modern city. Since Independence, Delhi has been flourishing as the capital of India. During the past decade, its population has increased exponentially, largely due to rapid economic expansion and increased job opportunities. The negative aspects of this boom are overcrowding, traffic congestion, shortage of dwellings, strain on city's infrastructure and pollution.

Today, Delhi manifests the symptoms of uncontrolled growth–distinct shortfalls in the infrastructural provisions of electricity, sewerage and water supply. Public transport facilities are inadequate. Unauthorized and uncontrolled land use, inadequate residential and commercial space, very high rates of rent, land grab, unbalanced growth and social compartmentalization are other problems the city faces. The Master Plan of Delhi (1962) was meant to prevent or contain these problems. However, these problems multiplied and new ones were added, such as air, water and noise pollution, rapidly dwindling green cover and degradation of the environment.

In Delhi, the proliferation of local bodies and fragmentation of micro-jurisdiction are equally pronounced. Various ministries and departments of the union government, the Delhi Development Authority, Town and Country Planning Organisation, Urban Arts Commission, National Capital Region Planning Board, MCD, NDMC, Delhi Transport Corporation, Delhi Jal Board, Vidyut Board, Delhi University, Cantonment Board, Railway Board and numerous other local agencies have their respective jurisdictions and functions. With so many authorities and due to the consequent overlapping of their jurisdiction, the common man experiences great difficulty in dealing with all of them with overlapping functions to deal with various civic or other problems. Further, these agencies operate under separate statutes, rules, regulations and orders. Each functional agency has its own scheme of decentralisation. The territorial boundaries of these divisions are not co-terminus, with the result that there is confusion and hardships to the people. In order to reduce overlapping, ensure effective control and make the functioning of various agencies and authorities more service-oriented for the common man, it has become imperative to make structural and functional changes in the existing set-up of Delhi's metropolitan area. This re-organisation, however has to ensure an efficient administrative set-up, considering the special status of Delhi as a national capital.

However, there are brighter sides of Delhi, which makes it so dear to its residents. Law and order here is better than that at other places in the country. The central part of it is beautifully planned, with a lot of greenery in its various pockets. Delhi is a cultural nerve centre of India. The cultural activity is at its best during the season from October to March when a host of dance and music are held performances from all parts of the country. Theatre is equally popular. It has one of the highest literacy rates in the country and provides good educational opportunities to the students. Its citizens are intellectually and politically active. Delhi is a place for every person to hone his skills. It has a rich tradition. Hand embroidery in silver and gold threads on silk and other fabrics have been going on for the past hundreds of years. Delhi is a gourmet's delight; it offers a variety of cuisines in its large number of restaurants. It is not a dry state. It has all the facilities, needed for a traveler or tourist. It has a range of accommodation in various star-category hotel. Since Delhi is a melting pot of those people who have migrated from all over the country and abroad, its culture as well as its social and occupational milieu reflects this confluence. Delhi is well connected to all the parts of the country through road, rail and air routes. However, being a landlocked city, it has no port. Citizens of all the countries (except Nepal, Bhutan and Maldives) need to have valid passports and an entry, transit or tourist visa. This visa can be obtained from the Indian Mission in their country before coming to Delhi.

▌ INFORMATION AT A GLANCE ▌

Status	Union Territory with a state assembly and Chief Minister
Area	1483 sq. kms.
Population (2011 census)	1,67,87,941 (Males: 89,87,326; Females: 78,00,615)
Density (persons per sq.km.)	11,320
Urban Population	97.50%.
Sex Ratio	868 females per 1000 males
Literacy	86.2%.
Sea Level Elevation	225 m (741 ft.)
Geographical location	Between 28° 24'-17" & 28° 53'-00" of North Latitude Between 76° 50'-24" and 77° 20'-37" of East Longitude.
Maximum Length	51.90 kms.
Maximum Breadth	48.48 kms
Surrounding Areas	District Ghaziabad in the east, District Rohtak in the west, District Sonepat in the north and District Gurugram in the south.
Principal Languages	Hindi, English, Punjabi & Urdu
Administrative Districts	11 (with 33 sub divisions)
Parliamentary Constituencies	7
Assembly Constituencies	70
Corporation Wards	272
Police Districts	13
Per Capita Income at Current Prices	₹ 3,65,529 (2018-19)

International Airport	Indira Gandhi International Airport is at a distance of about 20 kms (12 miles) due south-west of the city centre.
Domestic Airport	1
STD Code	011
Postal Code	1100XX
Time Zone	IST (4TC + 5:30)
Other Airports	Safdarjung Airport
River	Yamuna
Sea Port	None
Road Length	33,198 kms.
Length of National Highways	430 kms
Export Processing Zones	None
Major Industries	Manufacture of Razor Blades, Sports Goods, Radio & T.V. Parts, Plastic & PVC Goods, Textiles, Chemicals, Fertilizers, Soft Drinks, Hand & Machine Tools, Leather Goods, Galvanising & Electro-plating, Printing and Warehousing.
Crops	Wheat, Maize, Bajra, Jowar, Vegetables & Fruit Crops
Minimum Temperature	4°–5°C
Maximum Temperature	40°–45°C
Average Rainfall	714 mm
General Climate	Hot and Dry During Summer (April-June); Cold and Dry During Winter, (November-February); Wet and Humid during Rains (July-September); Dry and Warm During Autumn (September-October).

❑ ❑ ❑

History

2

DELHI is the custodian of a great heritage and has been cradle of many great civilizations. It has a glorious history of its own and has a rich and eventful past, being the capital of several empires.

■ THE CITIES OF DELHI ■

Delhi, as a full-fledged, prosperous and major city, took shape during the early medieval period. During the centuries that followed, it changed its locations several times but remained in existence as a living city. Rapid developments gave birth to cities (or capitals) in this area in a row, which are known in history as Seven Cities of Delhi.

FIRST CITY : INDRAPRASTHA

The earliest record of Delhi is found in the Hindu epic Mahabharata, which mentions a city called Indraprastha. The city was built in 1400 B.C. and located somewhere between the sites where the historic Old Fort (Purana Qila) and Humayun's Tomb exist, under the direction of Yudhisthira, the Pandava king. The excavations in 1955 within the old fort revealed that the area was inhabited even 3,000 years ago.

The first reference to the name Delhi seems to have been made during 1st century B.C. when Raja Dehlu built the first city of Delhi near the site where Qutab Minar is located at present. From the eighth century AD to ninth century AD, this city was the capital of Tomar Rajputs, who ruled a large part of northern India. The rulers had built a citadel, which they called Lal Kot, whose remains still exist in some form or the other in the area known as Mehrauli. In fact, Lal Kot was the first Delhi of the known history, which was known as Dilli. Later, the Chauhan Rajputs from Rajputana captured the town and preferred to call it Dehlu, even as the Lal Kot remained intact. In addition, Prithvi Raj Chauhan got constructed a new fort there, which he named Rai Pithora Durg (fort). It was he who had erected the famous iron pillar, which still exists near Qutab Minar and attracts visitors from all over the world.

SECOND CITY : SIRI

In around 1311 A.D., Allaudin Khilji established the second city at Siri and dug a vast reservoir at Hauz Khas, which is located at a distance of three miles due north of Qutab Minar. Remnants of fort Siri are hardly visible but Hauz Khas has been extensively renovated.

THIRD CITY : TUGHLAKABAD

Tughlakabad fort was built in 1321 as a protection against raiding Mangols. Built by Ghiyas-ud-Din Tughluq, it had to be abandoned in favour of the old site near Qutab Minar because of scarcity of water. The ruins of Tughlakabad are located near the present-day Delhi-Haryana border towards Faridabad.

FOURTH CITY : JAHANPANAH

Ghiyas-ud-Din Tughluq's successor, Muhammed bin Tughluq, extended the city towards the north-east and built new fortifications around it. It then, became the fourth city of Delhi, under the name Jahanpanah. The new settlements were located between the old cities near Qutab Minar and Siri Fort.

FIFTH CITY : FIRUZABAD

In 1354, Firuz Shah Tughluq abandoned this site and moved his capital further north towards the ancient site of Indraprastha. Thus, the fifth city of Delhi, Firuzabad, was founded on what is now the Firoz Shah Kotla area. Timur attacked Delhi in 1398 and ruthlessly destroyed it.

In 1526, Babur, the first Mughal ruler, re-established Delhi as the seat of his empire. His son, Humayun, built a new city on the site of the previously demolished Firuzabad and called it Din Panah. The Ashokan Pillar and Lodi Gardens are some of the monumental sites of this city.

SIXTH CITY : SHER SHAHI

Sher Shah, who overthrew Humayun in 1540, razed Din Panah and built his capital, the Sher Shahi (the Old Fort or Purana Qilah), as the sixth city of Delhi. Near this fort, are some of the places worth visiting, like Zoo, Crafts, Museum and the Pragati Maidan (exhibition grounds). The magnificient, Humayun Tomb, the precursor to the famous Taj Mahal, is located at a distance of about 2 km from here.

SEVENTH CITY : SHAHJAHANABAD

Delhi once again lost importance when Mughal emperors, Akbar (1556-1605) and Jahangir (1605-1627), moved their headquarters to Fatehpur Sikri and Agra, respectively. The city was restored to its glory in 1638, when the son of Jahangir, Shahjahan, laid the foundations of the seventh city of Delhi. It was Christened Shahjahanabad. He built a new, magnificent and large city along with a sprawling Red Fort and a grand Jama Masjid. He also built other buildings and a number of market places, including the famous Chandni Chowk. The present Old Delhi confined within the space of Shahjahan's walls and gates is what was known as Shahjahanabad. The famous Kashmiri Gate, Delhi Gate, Turkman Gate and the Ajmeri Gate, which were built during that century, still stand.

The fall of the Mughal empire during the mid-18th century made the city of Delhi witness many invasions and power changes. Although the East India Company first captured Delhi in 1803, yet the British assumed full control of the town only in 1858, when India came under the British Crown. The Britishers had already occupied Calcutta as their capital, which lasted till 1912. In 1912, the seat of power returned to Delhi. Initially, the British rulers built their capital due north of Shahjehanabad, where the old secretariat and other buildings constructed by them still exist and house the administrative offices of the city government. The British twisted Dilli to be spelt and pronounced as Delhi. But the city of Delhi, developed by the British, was not a new city. It was, in fact, merely an extension of the city of Shahjahan.

Following the rise and fall of the ancient cities and different Dillis, the British rulers felt the need for making a new, planned and modern city, to be used as its capital, to suit the new requirements. For that purpose, a new site, on Raisina hills, due south of Shahjehanabad, was selected and the task of planning a new city—in a very perfect manner—was assigned to Sir Edwin Lutyens. The new capital city, Christened as New Delhi, was inaugurated in 1931 and went on to become the seat of power in the British India. Later, it became the national capital of independent India.

IMPORTANT YEARS FOR DELHI

100 BC	Raja Dillu founded 'Dilli'
1151 AD	Chauhans captured Delhi
1192 AD	Mohammed Ghauri captured Delhi

1200 AD	First storey of Qutab Minar built
1305 AD	Hauz Khas built
1354 AD	Firuzabad built
1489 AD	Moth Ki Masjid built
1517 AD	Tomb of Sikander Lodi built
1538 AD	Dinpanah (Purana Kila) built
1565 AD	Humayun's Tomb built
1648 AD	Capital shifted to Shahjahanabad
1724 AD	Jantar Mantar built
1803 AD	The British took over Delhi
1857 AD	Siege of Delhi in the First Mutiny
1911 AD	Coronation Durbar in Delhi
1931 AD	The city of New Delhi inaugurated
1947 AD	India became independent
1950 AD	Delhi made the capital of the Republic
1962 AD	Master plan for Delhi drawn up
1985 AD	National Capital Region demarcated
1992 AD	Delhi got an Assembly and a Chief Minister

PREHISTORIC REFERENCES

Delhi is one of the most ancient cities of India. It has a recorded history of more than a thousand years. But the town was in existence even before that, perhaps for several thousand years. The earliest reference to a settlement at the site is to be found in the famous epic, Mahabharata. It was also known under the alternative names of Yoginipura and Khandava, which came into the possession of the Pandavas after the division of their ancestral estate by Dhritarashtra, their blind uncle. It further relates how the Pandavas led by Lord Krishna, expelled or subdued the savage Nagas and Takshakas, the original inhabitants of the place, cleared the forest and built the city of Indraprastha. According to eminent archaeologists, the date of the occupation of Indraprastha by Yudhishthira may be assigned to the fifth century B.C. The area where the famous Purana Qila built by Humayun and Sher Shah stands, is believed to be the site of Indraprastha. Some scholars are of the view that Indraprastha was bound by Meerut in the north, Gadavarta in the south, Mathura in the east and Dwarka in the west.

FIRST HISTORIC REFERENCE

As per the recorded history, it may be accepted that Delhi was founded in 736 A.D. by the Tomars, a clan of the Rajputs, whose kingdom bordered those of the Chahamanas of Sakambhari on the east. Perhaps, because of the threat of the attack of the Turks, Anangpal, the Tomar ruler of Delhi, had built a fort which was most likely Lal Kot. Constructed in the 11th century at a place where the Quwwatul Islam mosque now stands, it is said to be the first regular defence work in Delhi. Anangpal is also believed to have brought to Delhi and installed in the Lal Kot, in the fourth century, the standard of God Vishnu. The Tomars seem to have ruled Delhi till the middle of the twelfth century.

CHAUHAN RAJPUT RULERS

The Tomars were overthrown by the Chahamana, king, Vigraharaj IV Visaldeva (1153-63 A.D.). During his reign, the Chahamanas (Chauhans) established, for the first time, a large empire, extending up to the Shivalik hills in Saharanpur (U.P). The greatest monarch of this dynasty was his nephew, Prithviraj Chauhan (or Rai Pithora). During his reign (1179-92 A.D.), the fort of Lal Kot was further strengthened with the help of an exterior wall. Prithviraj was the last Hindu ruler of Delhi.

CONQUEST OF DELHI

In 1191 A.D., came the first invasion of Mohammed Shihabuddin Ghori. Though he was defeated by Prithviraj on this occasion, the Muslim adventurer returned the very next year with a reorganised force to avenge his defeat. He routed the Rajputs in the great battle of Tarain in 1192. Prithviraj was arrested and killed. Ghori captured Ajmer, the capital of Prithviraj. Ghori's forces also defeated Khande Rao, Prithviraj's brother and the Governor of Delhi and conquered Delhi. Ghori handed over Delhi to Qutubuddin (1206-10 A.D.), one of his generals. The possession of Delhi in those days did not mean much as its was neither the capital of India nor an important town.

FOUNDATION OF SULTANATE

Qutubuddin Aibak was the real founder of the Turkish dominion in India. In 1194, he erected the Quwwatul Islam (Might of Islam) mosque and started the construction of the famous Qutub Minar, probably as a tower of victory. It was completed by Iltutmish (1211-36), his son-in-law and successor, who formally made Delhi the capital of the Muslim empire. He also undertook some construction task at Lal Kot and further extended the size of the Quwwatul Islam mosque. Raziya (1236-39), who succeeded her father Iltutmish, is the only Muslim woman who ascended the throne of Delhi. Her reign was, however, shortlived. She fell a victim to the intrigues of the nobles. Raziya Sultana was succeeded by her brother, Nasiruddin Mehmood, a pious and gentle ruler.

MOST POWERFUL OF THE SLAVE SULTANS

Balban (1263-87), the most important ruler of the Slave dynasty, restored internal peace, raised the prestige of the crown and protected the Sultanate from Mangol attacks by making admirable arrangements for the defence of the north-western frontier. Balban's grandson Kaiqubad (1287-90), the son of Bughra Khan, succeeded him. Soon after his accession, he shifted to his newly built palace on the bank of Yamuna around, which the capital of Kilokari grew up.

THE KHILJI DYNASTY

The Slave dynasty was brought to an end by Jalaluddin Khilji who ascended the throne in 1290. He was a great warrior. This benevolent ruler was, however, treacherously murdered in 1296, by his nephew, Alauddin Khilji. Alauddin's reign marks the peak of Delhi. He assumed the title of Khalifah. Delhi, henceforth, came to be known as Dar-ul-Khalifah (seat of Caliph). He subjugated the Deccan and captured most of its territories. So, he brought almost the whole of the Indian subcontinent under his sway.

Delhi had become more of a fortified Turkish camp than a capital under the Slave kings. But under the rule of the Khiljis, it became the effective metropolis of India. Such literary figures as the poet Hazrat Amir Khusrau and Amir Hasan of Delhi adorned the court, which attracted scholars from far and wide. Alauddin's architectural taste manifested in his famous building, the Ala-i-Darwaza, which is claimed to be the most beautiful and perfect specimen of early Turkish architecture. In the new suburb of Siri, he built a hall of one thousand pillars. He protected this hall with lofty walls to protect it from the repeated Mangol invasions. The construction of Hauz Khas, the special tank and the unfinished *minar* which he had commenced to outmatch the Qutab Minar, stands as a testimony to his great designs.

THE TUGHLAK DYNASTY

After a brief period of instability following the death of Alauddin, Ghiyasuddin Tughlaq, the Governor of Punjab, occupied the Delhi throne in 1320. Just after taking over the reigns of power, Ghiyasuddin decided to lay the foundation of a fortified town, called Tughlakabad. It was located five miles due east of the city in a highly defensive position on the edge of the rocky hills, which stretch from Badarpur to Faridabad. His main palace, all traces of which are now lost, is said to have been built of gilded bricks, which used to shine so brilliantly in the Sun that none could gaze steadily upon it. The Sultans's death is ascribed to the complicity of Prince Juna Khan, who later ascended the throne as Mohammed Bin Tughlak (1325-51).

THE WISE AND INSANE KING

Mohammed Bin Tughlak has been described as "one of the most accomplished princes and most furious tyrants that ever adorned or disgraced human nature." He was the author of many a grandiose plans such as the introduction of token currency. Another such plan was the transfer of the capital from Delhi to Devagiri, renamed Daulatabad, 700 miles away in the Deccan, which, in his opinion, had a more central position. The people of Delhi were reluctant to move. Tughluk issued a proclamation, ordering the residents to leave Delhi within three days. And the order was strictly enforced. In spite of the excellent arrangements made by the Sultan for the comfort of the travellers, people of Delhi suffered tremendously. Many died on their way to the new capital and many after reaching the destination. As soon as the Sultan realised the failure of his project, he ordered the people to leave Daulatabad and return to their homes in Delhi. He even asked the inhabitants of other cities to move into Delhi to add to its population. But Delhi could only partially be made populous and could not regain its former glory for many years to come.

A GREAT BUILDER

Feroze Shah Tughlak (1351-88), who succeeded Mohammed bin Tughlak, was essentially a man of peace and devoted his energies towards improving the lot of the people. Feroze Tughlak is worthy of remembrance as the maker of a canal from Yamuna to the dry countryside, which was located due west of Delhi. In this area, he founded the town known as Hisar-e-Firuzah or Ferozabad. Ferozabad (or Feroze Shah Kotla), his new capital, is at a distance of about eight miles due north of Qutub Minar. But it did not mark the transfer of the capital to the new site. Thus, there were two cities flourishing at the same time, the old Delhi at Qutab and the new city at Ferozabad.

After Feroze's death, within ten years, five kings ascended the throne of Delhi, one after the other. The last one of them was Mahmud Tughlak (1395-1413); his reign lasted for 18 years.

TIMUR'S ATTACK

Timur reached Delhi in the first week of December, 1398. He was opposed by the forces of Mahmud. The Delhi army fought bravely but was defeated and Mahmud fled to Gujarat. One to the oppressive conduct of Timur's soldiers, people of the city were forced to offer resistance. Thereupon, Timur ordered a general plunder and massacre, which lasted for several days. Timur also picked up some of the expert artisans of Delhi and sent them to Samarkand to build for him the famous grand mosque. After remaining in Delhi for a fortnight, Timur marched back. Timur left Delhi prostrate and bleeding; trade, commerce and other signs of material prosperity disappeared; the city was depopulated and ruined. There was scarcity and severe famine in the capital and its suburbs. For about three months after the departure of Timur, Delhi virtually remained without inhabitants. The kingdom of Delhi had now shrunk to the dimensions of a petty principality, comprising the capital city and a few districts around it. Mahmud returned but was unable to recover his lost territories and, after an ineffectual reign, he died in 1413. His death brought the Tughlak dynasty to an end.

THE SAYYED DYNASTY

The nobles of Delhi nominated Daulat Khan, an influential noble, to the throne. But Khizr Khan, the Governor of Punjab, who had helped Timur and was a Sayyed, drove out Daulat Khan and founded the Sayyed dynasty in May, 1414. Khizr Khan maintained the independence of his kingdom against the incursions of the kings of Jaunpur and Gujarat, who wanted to annex Delhi. Nothing of importance happened during the reigns of his three successors-Mubarak Shah (1421-34). Mohammed Shah (1432-45) and Alauddin Alam Shah (1445-50).

THE LODI DYNASTY

After the brief rule by the Sayyed dynasty, Bahlol Lodi, the Governor of Punjab, seized Delhi after a coup in 1450 and laid the foundation of Lodi dynasty. He was succeeded by his son Sikandar (1489-1517) who moved his capital to the neighbourhood of Agra and built a new city called Sikandarabad. The third and the last of the line, Ibrahim (1517-26) tried to impose a rigorous discipline and strict ceremonial rituals on his peers who resented these restrictions on their liberty and privileges. The tensions that followed, culminated into a rebellion. This confused state of affairs afforded an opportunity to Babar, a descendent of Timur, to invade India. Ibrahim's forces were defeated in the battle at Panipat (1526), thus ending the rule of the Lodi dynasty. And with this, the era of Delhi Sultanate also came to an end.

THE MUGHAL ERA

After defeating the last Lodi Sultan, the ambitious and courageous king of Kabul, Zahiruddin Mohammed Babar, entered Delhi in 1526 but he spent most of his time at Agra only. He died in 1530, leaving a large but unstable kingdom, which extended from Kabul in the west to the borders of Bengal in the east. His son and successor, Humayun (1530-40 and 1555-56), was perplexed about the choice of his capital. He had two cities to choose from—Delhi and Agra. Ultimately, he tried to restore or build a fort, called Din-panah on the site of the ancient Indraprastha. The name, however, soon fell into disuse and the fort came to be known as Purana Qila, which still exists.

SHER SHAH'S RULE

The reign of Humayun was broken into two parts by an interlude of 15 years. During this period, the Sur dynasty was founded by the Afghan monarch, Sher Shah in 1540. He established his supremacy in most of the parts of northern India. The battles of Chausa in 1539 and Kannauj in 1540 decided against Humayun, who had to take refuge after his defeat. Sher Shah, immediately after his accession in 1540, took steps to improve the administration of Delhi. He made addition to the Purana Qila and founded a city which extended from the fort of Kotla Feroze Shah to the area around Purana Qila. Sher Shah is, however, remembered by posterity, not for the buildings he constructed, but for his contribution in the fields of civil administration. After a brief reign of five years, this great ruler died. His successors were not up to the mark and their inability led to their downfall. During this period of violence and anarchy, Delhi suffered terribly. A severe famine broke out, which took a heavy toll of lives in the city.

HUMAYUN'S RETURN

Humayun, taking advantage of the situation, attacked and regained the throne of India in 1555. Humayun's position was, however, far from secure. Hemu, the general of Mohammed Adil Shah, had arrived at

Tughlakabad with a huge army. Hemu took possession of the city, assuming the title of Raja Vikramjit. He, thus, became the first and the only Hindu to occupy the throne of Delhi during the Medieval period. However, before any decisive battle could be fought, Humayun died after a fall from the steep stairs of his library in Purana Qila and his minor son, Akbar, was crowned as the emperor of India in 1556. Akbar's forces, led by his guardian, Bairam Khan, met those of Hemu at Panipat. In the battle that ensured, Hemu was defeated.

DELHI UNDER AKBAR

During Akbar's reign, the city of Delhi formed a part of the Suba of Delhi, comprising eight sarkars and subdivided into 232 paraganas. It extended from Palwal to Ludhiana on one side, from Rewari to Kumaon hills on the other and from Hisar to Khizrabad on the third. During Akbar's reign, Delhi was of secondary importance.

DELHI: A RUINED CITY

Fifty years of reign of Akbar were followed by the accession of his son, Jahangir, who reigned for 22 years (1605-27). Besides Agra, he made his headquarters for some time at Lahore as well. Delhi was one of the 15 provinces under Jahangir and a Subedar used to be the in-charge of this area. A bubonic plague broke out during his reign. It took a heavy toll of the lives in Delhi (1616-24).

IMPERIAL CAPITAL AGAIN

The next Moghul ruler, Shahjahan, decided to build his capital at Delhi; it was to be equipped with a citadel and royal residence. Shahjahanabad, the new city, soon grew around it with a number of fine palaces built by the nobles and merchants. Shahjahan also built the famous Jama Masjid. In order to build the walls of his capital, Shahjahan pulled down what was left of Ferozabad and the city of Sher Shah Suri.. The famous Peacock Throne was brought from Agra. It was during Shahjahan's reign that the power and the wealth of the Mughal Empire and the splendour of its court reached the zenith. Thus, Delhi became the premier city of India and also, in importance during the whole of Asia. In 1657, Shahjahan fell ill and was taken to Agra by his eldest son, Dara Shikoh. Shahjahan was deposed in 1658 by his third son Aurangzeb, who had emerged triumphant out of the struggle for power among the four sons of the emperor.

AURANGZEB'S REGIME

An event of, the reign of Aurangzeb was the execution of the Sikh Guru Ji, Tegh Bahadur, at Delhi. The trunk of the banyan tree under which, Guru Tegh Bahadur was beheaded in 1675, can still be seen within the precincts of Gurudwara Sisganj in Chandni Chowk. Delhi maintained its importance during the reign of Aurangzeb, though he spent most of his time in fighting wars against the Marathas and the kingdoms Deccan.

THE DECLINE OF MUGHALS

With the death of Aurangzeb in 1707, began the rapid decline of the Mughal Empire. There were quick successions to the throne for which, struggles were unending and during which, Delhi suffered much and quite often. Azam Shah, Bahadur Shah, Jahandar Shah, Farrukhsiyar and Mohammed Shah became rulers in quick succession during this period of decline.

THE MARATHA ONSLAUGHT

It was during the reign of Mohammed Shah that the Marathas, under Peshwa, Baji Rao, came to Delhi and fought a battle against the Mughal rulers at a place near Talkatora. The Marathas were victorious. However, Baji Rao did not sack Delhi and retired.

MASSACRE BY NADIR SHAH

On February 24, 1739, Nadir Shah, the emperor of Persia (Iran), defeated the Mughal troops at Karnal. Emperor Mohammed Shah surrendered to the invader. The keys of the fortress, treasury and store houses were handed over to Nadir Shah's messengers. Incensed over the killing of his soldiers by the citizens of Delhi, Nadir Shah ordered the slaughter and plundering of the city. By the time, Nadir Shah ordered his soldiers to refrain from further slaughter, thousands of people had been killed. Estimates vary from 8000 to 400000. The streets of Delhi were littered with corpses. A famine also broke out. Nadir Shah then, turned his attention to extortion and plunder. Contributions were levied upon all, rich and poor, and extorted by every possible means. The famous Peacock Throne and the invaluable Koh-i-Noor diamond were among Nadir's prized possessions before he finally rode out of Delhi on May 16, 1739.

THE CIVIL WAR

Mughal Empire, however, soon recovered from the shock of Nadir's invasion. Mohammed Shah was still occupying the throne. The court rivalries, however, continued unabated. They took a serious turn after the death of Mohammed Shah in 1748. His son and successor, Ahmad Shah ruled for six years before Safdarjung grabbed power. During Safdarjung's rule, the city of Delhi suffered terribly due to the civil war. Safdarjung invited the Jat ruler, Suraj Mal (of Bharatpur), who plundered Delhi recklessly. Safdarjung was ousted from power by Itmad-ul-Mulk who requested the Marathas for help. Malhar Rao Holkar attacked the Imperial Camp at Sikanderabad in 1754, crossed the Yamuna and plundered Jaisinghpura. The Marathas were persuaded to desist from taking a further action, Ahmad Shah was deposed and Mohammed Aziz-ud-din was raised to the throne as Alamgir II.

INVASIONS OF ABDALI

Even as Delhi was passing through the turbulent period, the news of the arrival of the Afghan invader, Ahmed Shah Abdali came in 1757. There began an exodus from the capital and when Abdali reached Delhi, there was no defender or caretaker. Abdali was determined to realise the spoils of war as quickly as possible and he spared neither the royal family nor the common man. Najib Khan the Rohilla chief, was left by Abdali as his chief agent in Delhi. Finding the time to be opportune, the Marathas demanded Chauth, a part of the revenue from the emperor as they had been getting during the reigns of Mohammed Shah and his son the land areas assigned to them held Alamgir II responsible for the payment. After the emperor's reply of inability to meet their demand, the Maratha forces marched upon Delhi and plundered the area. Najib Khan had no alternative but to surrender unconditionally.

RETURN OF ABDALI

Ahmed Shah Abdali soon returned in 1760.The Maratha army tried to engage his forces but fell in a battle that was fought at a distance of ten miles due north of Delhi. The victorious king encamped near Yamuna and appointed Yaqub Ali Khan as Subedar of Delhi and returned. The Marathas, under Sadashiv Bhau reappeared and began a regular siege of the fort. Yaqub Ali Khan had no alternative but to surrender the fort. Bhau deposed Shahjahan II and proclaimed Shah Alam as the emperor. It seems that Delhi was destined to fall prey alternately to Abdali and the Marathas. Ahmed Shah Abdali finally defeated the Marathas at the battle of Panipat in 1761 and entered Delhi where he remained for a month and a half, held his court and grabbed as much money as he possibly could.

SHAH ALAM IN DELHI

Shah Alam, who was in exile at Allahabad, had joined a coalition of Mir Qasim and the Nawab of Awadh against the British but their combined forces were routed at Buxar. Under a treaty, the emperor had to formally grant the Diwani of Bengal, Bihar and Orissa to the East India Company. The English promised to restore the emperor to his capital. But when his repeated entreaties met with no response, Shah Alam turned towards the Marathas who readily agreed. Maratha forces captured the imperial capital on February 10, 1771. After extorting some concessions, they handed over the fort to the emperor's agent. Shah Alam rode into the capital in 1772. The Marathas, however, soon fell out with the emperor and attacked Delhi. In spite of the stiff resistance offered by the imperial troops, the Marathas were able to force their way into Delhi. Mahadji Scindia was appointed as the emperor's deputy as well as Commander-in-Chief. In fact, Scindia remained in northern India as the nominal slave but the rigid master of Shah Alam, the emperor of Delhi. During a brief period, the Rohilla Chief, Ghulam Qadir, seized Delhi in 1788. During this period, the royal family had to undergo great sufferings and its treasury and secret royal chambers were ransacked. The Marathas again came to the emperor's rescue and Shah Alam was retained as the emperor. For 13 long years, Delhi remained a Maratha province.

BRITISH CONTROL

Lord Wellesley, the Governor General of India from 1798 to 1805, wanted to make the British supreme in India. He fully realised the importance of the Mughal emperor as a great political asset and was determined to bring him under British control. When the Anglo-Maratha war broke out in 1803, the French General, who was Scindia's commandant of the Delhi fortress, pressed for money from the Qiladar. When his request was turned down, he started bombarding the fort. The frightened emperor sent a message to the British General, begging him to come to his rescue. The Marathas were defeated by the British in 1803 in the battle at Patparganj.

DELHI, A LARGE PROVINCE

In 1803, Delhi was declared to be a non-regulated area, the rule being that the spirit of regulations was to be observed as far as circumstances permitted. Delhi soon acquired importance as the frontier capital of the rapidly growing British empire in India. In fact, Delhi formed a province of its own; its territory was not simply the city and the surrounding country. Besides the assigned territories and the *Jagir* of Rampur, it contained Rohelkhand, (districts of Bareilly, Moradabad and Shahjehanpur), Meerut, Haryana, Sirhind, Patiala and various small Sikh states.

A SHADOW RULER

Although the British respected the dignity of the Mughal emperor of Delhi, yet they treated him as a shadow ruler. The emperor's domain was reduced by the appropriation of all the portions of the territories situated on the right bank of river Yamuna. In lieu of this, the British made a provision of Rs. 90000 per month for the maintenance of the royal family. The Mughal emperor's powers were further curtailed when the British resident took upon himself the duties of collection of revenues and the administration of justice. The civil and criminal jurisdiction of the emperor was now limited only to the four walls of the royal palace. The succeeding British Governor Generals kept on reducing the powers of the Mughal emperor and also made him plainly see that he was a mere shadow. His request for an increase in the stipend was turned down. The emperor deputed Raja Ram Mohan Roy to advocate his case in England but with little success. He was also refused to confer honorary titles as he had been doing earlier.

THE LAST MONARCH

Akbar Shah II was succeeded by Sirajuddin Mohammed Zafar who took the title of Bahadur Shah (1837-57). His interests were primarily literary and aesthetic. In his court, flourished two great Urdu poets— Ghalib and Zauq. This peace-loving monarch had to face many problems. The British government looked upon the emperor as a source of potential danger to their rule in India. They were keen to divest him of all the vestiges of the royal authority. Under a conspiracy, the eldest surviving son of the king, Mirza Kobash, was recognised as the heir-apparent (1856), as he had agreed to the designation and position of prince or *Shahzada* instead of the title of emperor, to the great resentment of all other princes.

FIRST WAR OF INDEPENDENCE

Although the first shots of the great revolt of 1857 were fired at Meerut on May 10, yet on the morning of May 11, the Indian troops entered Delhi. Its residents were unaware of the outbreak of the revolt at Meerut and the news came as a great surprise to the emperor as well as the British officers. The palace guards offered no resistance and most of the senior British officials were murdered. The rebels refused to listen to the overtures of the emperor and called upon him in the name of religion to assume their command. It was after a good deal of hesitation that he finally decided to throw his lot with the revolutionaries. There were no European troops at hand and the Indian soldiers in the British army refused to fire on their brethren even when their officers were massacred. Rather, the sepoys opened fire on their own officers, who had to flee to save their lives. The massacre of Europeans and Indian Christians went on in the city. By the night, the soldiers were the sole masters within the city walls and every vestige of British authority had been removed. Historians describe the Act of Soldiers and rulers as the first war of independence.

NO ORDER

The condition of the city was chaotic. Antisocial elements were quite active and arson and loot was indiscriminately resorted to. The awful state of affairs continued till May 12, when the emperor decided to restore order. Soldiers, young and old, trained and untrained, kept pouring in from all parts of the country to take part in the war against the British. But there was no space, ration or ammunition for them. The soldiers could not be paid as there was no money in the treasury. Those soldiers, who could not get their meals for days together, took to plunder. The emperor, on his part, had no good feeling for the warring troops who were practically not under his control.

DELHI UNDER SIEGE

The British regarded the recovery of Delhi as an act of supreme importance for restoring their shattered prestige. They were prepared to sacrifice everything to achieve this object. The British troops, which left Meerut on May 27, under the command of Brigadier Wilson, were opposed by the Indian soldiers who had occupied a strong position on the banks of the Hindon river, at a distance of 20 miles from Delhi. The Indian forces led by Mirza Abu Bakr, one of the king's sons, were defeated. Wilson was thus, able to join his forces with those of Sir

Bernard at Alipur, at distance of 12 miles from Delhi, on June 7. The troops under the command of Mirza Khizr Sultan, another of the king's sons, entrenched themselves at a place called Badli-ki-sarai, about five miles to the north-west of Delhi. The British made a frontal attack but met with stiff resistance. The Indians retreated under pressure but inflicted heavy casualties on the enemy. The British pushed forward and occupied the Ridge, a place of great strategic importance, for it commanded the whole of the city of Delhi. Sir Bernard prepared his forces for a long siege. The Indians carried out a number of sorties and attacked the British from the front and the rear ends but without any success. With the arrival of fresh reinforcements from Punjab, the strength of the British forces at the Ridge increased. The Indian army had also been greatly strengthened with the arrival of the Bareilly contingent under General Bakht Khan on July 1 and 2, 1857. General Khan assumed command of the fighting forces. A fierce battle ensued in which, the Indian troops fought valiantly but the rout was complete. The British forces kept on advancing on every street became a barricade and bullets and stones were hurled on every inch of the ground was fought for and there were hundreds of casualties. Finally, the British forces succeeded in capturing the fort on September 20 without any difficulty. Everybody found in the fort was shot dead. The emperor had already retired with his family to the Qutab.

THE LAST DAY OF THE EMPIRE

Bahadur Shah and his queen surrendered to Hudson on September 21. Next day, the British arrested the princes-Mirza Mughal, Khizr Sultan and Mirza Abu Bakr. Soon after, they were killed near the Khooni Darwaza,. Twenty-one princes of the royal family were hanged a little later. The Raja of Ballabhgarh and Nawabs of Gurgaon, Jhajjar and Farrukhnagar met the same fate. Bahadur Shah was tried by a military court for rebellion and complicity in the murder of Europeans. The court declared him guilty on all counts and he was exiled to Rangoon with his favourite wife. There, he died on November 7, 1862.

THE CITY OF GHOSTS

The massacre at Delhi and the state of affairs after the capture of the city was dreadful. The way from the Lahori Gate by the Chandni Chowk led through a veritable city of the dead; not a single living creature was to be seen. Famous bazaars were destroyed beyond recognition. All the important mosques, viz., Jama Masjid, Masjid

Fatehpuri and Masjid Kalan were, occupied by the British forces. Jama Masjid was restored to the Muslims only after about five years on making a payment of Rs. 2 lakh in cash. Orders were issued, asking the people to quit the city. The whole city was given to plunder. Nearly 1400 residents were marched to the Yamuna where they were beheaded and their bodies were thrown in the river. Thus, lawlessness, murder and rapes went on for several days. A military court tried hundreds of people, many of whom were sent to the gallows. Even the places of worship were not spared from loot. Thus, there remained nothing but bare walls and empty houses in Delhi. The residents, whose number had been considerably reduced due to the vagaries of cold and starvation, were asked to return after paying a fine.

PEACE RESTORED AT LAST

The city was finally handed over to the civil authorities on January 11, 1858. The events of 1857 brought the Company's rule to an end. India was henceforth, to be governed by and in the name of Her Majesty the Queen of England. The seat of the government remained at Calcutta and Delhi was relegated to a secondary position. During this period of oblivion, Delhi retained its importance mainly as a centre of the cultural life of northern India. Its historical monuments were another source of attraction. However, it is significant to note that Delhi was the venue chosen for all the three memorable Durbars held in subsequent years.

THE ROYAL DURBARS

Lord Lytton (1876-80) held a magnificent Durbar in January, 1877 at Delhi to celebrate the assumption of the title of Kaiser-i-Hind (Empress of India) by Queen Victoria of England. The venue of the Durbar was the ground along the historic ridge. Twenty-six years later, on January 1, 1903, the Viceroy, Lord Curzon (1899-1905), arranged the second Durbar at Delhi to proclaim Edward VII as the King Emperor. This Durbar was, no doubt planned on the model of the Durbar of 1877 but it was on a much larger and more gorgeous scale. The presence of the Duke and Duchess of Connaught lent colour to the ceremony. The investiture ceremony took place in the historic building of Diwan-i-Am in the Red Fort, while Diwan-i-Khas, converted into a super room with a covered passage, was used for the State Ball. Finally, the third and most magnificent Durbar was held on December, 12, 1911. At this grand Durbar, King George V announced the transfer of the seat of power from Calcutta to Delhi.

RETURN OF GLORY

The royal proclamation returned the status and glory of Delhi as the capital of India after five decades. The capital was finally moved to Delhi in 1912. And with this, Delhi, the historic city, began a new phase of its journey. First of all, it acquired the status of the capital of British India. Later, it became the national capital of independent India. Initially, the capital was located on the ridge due north of the walled city of Delhi. As this site was not found suitable to serve as the seat of the government, a gew city, namely, New Delhi, located due south of the walled city, was planned. Construction work of New Delhi started in 1912 under the supervision of the renowned city planners and architects, Sir Edwin Lutyens and Sir Herbert Baker. Construction of New Delhi was completed in 1931 when the seat of the Government was shifted to this new place.

When the British decided to make Delhi their capital, they built New Delhi in a grandiose imperial style, as if the Sun would never set on the British Raj. Only 16 years after the city was inaugurated as the nation's capital, India witnessed the trauma of partition. In a matter of weeks, Delhi was transformed from a Muslim-dominated city of less than a million inhabitants into a largely Hindu city of almost two million people. Today, very few city residents can claim that they are the 'real' *Delhi-wallahs*. Further, most of the population of New Delhi comprises refugees or migrants from other states. The city has continued to grow at a fast pace since the time of independence, which was granted to our nation on August 15, 1947.

❏ ❏ ❏

Places of Interest 3

▮ HISTORICAL MONUMENTS ▮

RED FORT

Delhi's most magnificent monument, the Red Fort, was built by Emperor Shahjahan, in 1638 A.D at an estimated cost of Rs 9 crores. Shahjehan, after reigning at Agra for 11 years, decided to transfer his capital again to Delhi. Some of the buildings the Red Fort encloses are 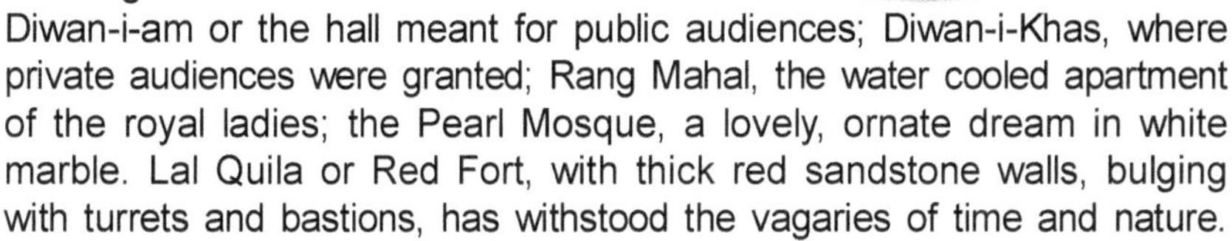 Diwan-i-am or the hall meant for public audiences; Diwan-i-Khas, where private audiences were granted; Rang Mahal, the water cooled apartment of the royal ladies; the Pearl Mosque, a lovely, ornate dream in white marble. Lal Quila or Red Fort, with thick red sandstone walls, bulging with turrets and bastions, has withstood the vagaries of time and nature.

The Lal Quila rises above a wide dry moat in the north-eastern corner of the original city of Shahjahanabad. This fort is an irregular octagonal building, with its two long sides on the east and west and six smaller ones on the north and south. Its circumference is about one-and-a-half mile; its length from north to south is 3200 feet and breadth from east to west is 1800 feet. The ditch around it is 75 feet wide and 30 feet deep, which was filled with water during war times.

> Red Fort was included in UNESCO'S World Heritage List on June 28, 2007.

The fort contains all the features of the Mughal architecture — halls of public and private audience, domed and arched marble palaces, plush private apartments, a mosque and elaborately designed gardens. No one can describe the grandeur of the fort during the days of Mughals as after that, it has undergone many vicissitudes. In 1719, the fort and its building were greatly damaged by earthquake shocks. In 1739, Nadir Shah carried away the famous Peacock Throne and the palace treasure to Persia. In 1759, serious havoc was wrought by Maratha and Jat assaults. In 1798, the dreadful Rohilla chieftain, Ghulam Qader, set fire to the fort. And finally, after the revolt of 1857, many gardens and buildings of the fort were demolished.

The famous Takht-e-Taus or the Peacock Throne was 5 feet by 4 feet in dimensions. It was made of golds and weighed 1 lakhs tolas. Its upper portion was inlaid with diamonds, and weighed rubies, emeralds, sapphires and other valuable gems and the lower one was made of gold, set with topazes. On an enamelled tree, one wonderful peacock, adorned with bright gems, was constructed. The canopy of the throne was also set with diamonds and a border of glorious pearls. Some fancy verses were written on it with green enamel. The throne was supported by twelve emerald-coloured stones. In order to ascend the throne, a beautiful silver staircase was prepared.

Entrance to the fort is through the imposing Lahori Gate, which takes its name from the fact that it faces Lahore, now in Pakistan. This gate has a special significance for India since the first war of independence was fought here. Further, important speeches were delivered here by freedom fighters and national leaders of India. The Delhi Gate is in its southern wall but is now closed to the general public. Besides, these there are three more gates and two more windows but of a little importance.

The main entrance opens on to the Chatta Chowk, a covered street flanked with arched cells that used to house Delhi's most talented jewellers, carpet makers, weavers and goldsmiths. This arcade was also known as the Meena Bazaar, the shopping centre for the ladies of the court. Just beyond the Chhata Chowk, is the heart of the fort called Naubat Khana or the Drum House. The musicians used to play for the emperor from the Naubat Khana and the arrival of princes and royalty was heralded from this place.

The fort also houses the Diwan-i-Am or the Hall of Public Audiences where the emperor used to sit and hear the complaints of the common folk. His alcove in the wall was marble-panelled and set with precious stones, many of which were looted after the mutiny of 1857. The Diwan-i-Khas is the hall of private audiences where the emperor used to hold private meetings. This hall is made of marble and its centre-piece used to be the Peacock Throne.

The other attractions within this monument are the Royal Baths or *hammams*, the Shahi Burj, which used to be Shahjahan's private working area and the Moti Masjid or the Pearl Mosque, built by Aurangzeb for his personal use. The Rang Mahal or the Palace of Colours used to house the emperor's wives and mistresses. This palace was crowned with gilded turrets, delicately painted and decorated with an intricate mosaic of mirrors. Its ceiling was overlaid with gold and silver that was reflected in a central pool in the marble floor.

Even today, the Lal Quila is an eloquent reminder of the glory of the Mughal era and its magnificence leaves many wonder-struck and breathless. It still transports the visitor to another era of time. A sound and light show, organised during evenings, recreates events in India's history that is connected with the fort.

JAMA MASJID

Built by emperor Shahjahan, it is an eloquent reminder of the Mughal religious fervour. Its spacious courtyard can hold thousands of devout Muslims. This monument was built between 1644 and 1658 by five thousand artisans. Originally called Masjid-i-Jahanuma, or "the mosque commanding the view of the world," this magnificent structure stands on the Bho Jhala, one of the two hills of the old Mughal capital city of Shahjahanabad. On the east, this monument faces the Lal Quila (Red Fort). The mosque includes three round domes (*gumbads*), three gateways, four towers, a central pond 40-metre and two high minarets. The main dome has a diameter of 40 feet while the other two have a diametre of 30 feet each. Interestingly, an underground tunnel, connecting the Red Fort with the Jama Masjid, was constructed to enable women from the royal family to reach the mosque in *purdah*. Also located in the courtyard, is a sundial (whose angle is now broken) and a world map, both of which, are engraved on three feet squares of white marble each. Having a unique construction of alternating vertical strips of red sandstone and white marble, the Jama Masjid is the largest and perhaps, the most magnificent mosque in India.

Broad flights of steps lead up to the imposing gateways in the north and the south. The main eastern entrance, probably used by the emperors, remains closed on most days of the week. The main prayer hall on the west side, faced by a series of high cusped arches and topped with marble domes, houses a niche in a wall that shelters the prayer leader. Worshippers use this hall on most days but on Fridays and other holy days, the courtyard is full of devotees who offer *namaaz*. Near the north gate of the mosque, stands a cupboard containing a collection of Prophet Muhammed's relics — *the Quran* written on deerskin, a red beard-hair of the prophet, his sandals and also his footprint, embedded in a marble slab.

QUTUB MINAR

This minar is the highest tower in India and dates back to the thirteenth century. It is one of the greatest bequests of the Islamic culture. Although the minar has been damaged by lightening and earthquakes, yet its magnificence fascinates the minds of the people coming from far and wide. At its base dating back to lies the Quwwatul-Islam Masjid, the first mosque in India. A famous iron pillar, the fifth century, stands before it. For 1500 years, it has remained rust free. According to a local belief the visitor if can get his fingers to touch, with his back to the pillar, his wishes will be granted.

The Qutab Minar is a soaring 73 metres (240-feet) high tower of victory, built in 1193 by Qutab-ud-din Aibak, immediately after the defeat of Delhi's last Hindu kingdom. However, in the days of Qutubuddin Aibak, the minar could not go beyond its first storey. It was his successor Shamsuddin Iltutmish who superimposed the second and third storeys upon it in 1210. Rest of the storeys with along with a cupola, were added by Feeroz Shah Tughlak in 1357. It is said that once the minar had seven storeys in all, attaining a height of 300 feet. But now thus, there are only five storeys, each marked by a projecting balcony. The minor tapers from a 15-metres (50-feet) diameter at the base to just 2.5-metres (8-feet) diameter at the top. The first three storeys are made of red sandstone, the fourth and fifth storeys are made of marble and sandstone. The stairs inside the tower coil so steeply that they can make the hardiest climber dizzy and claustrophobic. On the top of the fifth storey, there was a cupola, 12 ft. 10 in high. It was damaged by lightning and got repaired by Sikander Lodi in 1503. In 1803, the cupola was destroyed and thrown down by an earthquake. But it was again replaced by the British in 1828. Later, Lord Hardinge got it removed and now, it is placed near the Qutub Minar.

Earlier, people were allowed to climb on the top of the Qutab Minar to get a spectacular view of the countryside below it. But due to safety reasons, the authorities have now disallowed access on the minar. However, recently an electronically simulated system has been installed through which, one can feel as if the view was from one of the floors of the minar.

ALAI DARWAZA

At a small distance from the Qutub Minar, there stands a big gate, called Alai Darwaza. It was built of red sandstone, richly ornamented with design in relief by Alauddin Khilji in 1310. It is the most magnificent gate in the world. The planning of the gateway is in square measuring 35.6 ft. internally and 55.6 ft. externally. The height of the walls is 47 ft. from the floor to the ceiling and has a thickness of 11 feet. There are two windows closed by massive screens of marble lattice work at each corner of the building. Besides, there is the Alai minar whose construction was commenced by King Alauddin Khilji but could not be completed as the king had died in 1315. The height of this tower would have been 500 ft., had it been completed. Now its height is 70 ft. above the plinth, which is at a height of 37 ft. above the ground.

PURANA QUILA

Purana Qila is supposed to be the site of Indraprastha, the original city of Delhi built by the Pandavas. The Afghan ruler, Sher Shah, who briefly interrupted the Mughal empire by defeating Humayun, completed the fort during his reign during 1538-45. The fort, located due south-east of the India Gate and due north of the Nizamuddin railway station, has massive walls and three large gateways. There is a small octagonal tower made of red sandstone, called Sher Mandal, inside the fort near the South Gate. It was later used by Humayun as a library. On a day in 1556, while descending the stairs of this tower, he slipped, fell and received injuries due to which, he died. The Qila-i-Kuhran Mosque, or the Mosque of Sher Shah, lies just beyond it and unlike the fort itself, is in a fairly good condition. There is also a small archaeological museum just inside the main gate of the mosque.

SAFDARJANG'S TOMB

The tomb was built in 1753-54 by the Nawab of Avadh for his father, Safdarjang and is one of the last examples of the Mughal architecture before the final remnants of the great empire collapsed. The tomb stands on a high terrace in an extensive garden. Its central hall supports a dome with marble minarets. It is a 900-feet. square of three storeys, with fawn-coloured stonework. In the central chamber, is the carved cenotaph and in the chamber below, are two earth graves.

JANTAR MANTAR

It is an astronomical observatory with masonry instruments. It was built in 1724 by the Rajput king of Jaipur, Sawai Jai Singh, the mathematician and astronomer king for observing the movements of the stars and planets. The Samrat Yantra or the Supreme Instrument, the largest structure shaped like a right-angled triangle, is actually a huge sun-dial; the other five instruments in its vicinity are intended to show the movements of the sun, moon etc. It is a remarkable monument of scientific and historic value.

SHAHJAHANABAD

The most splendid of Delhi's old cities, built by emperor Shahjehan, is now a part of old Delhi. It was surrounded by a wall, which is 8.8 kms in circumference terms of 14 massive gates. It has ;5 of these still stand — Delhi Gate, Kashmere Gate, Turkman Gate, Ajmeri Gate and Lahori Gate.

FEROZSHAH KOTLA

It is the site of the city of Ferozabad, built during the fourteenth century by emperor Ferozshah Tughlaq. The famed 14-meter-high polished sandstone Ashoka Pillar, carrying emperor Ashoka's message of peace stands here today and is nearly 2,300 years old. The rest of the structures, including the Wazir's house near the northern wall Zanana Mahal (palace for ladies) and Diwan-i-Khas are lying in heaps of ruins.

HUMAYUN'S TOMB

It was built by Humayun's widow Queen Haji Begum, during the sixteenth century.The remains of the emperor were removed from the Old Fort, where he had died in 1556 and buried at the place where those now lie. From an architectural viewpoint, it is the forerunner of the Taj Mahal. It stands at Nizamuddin. Its 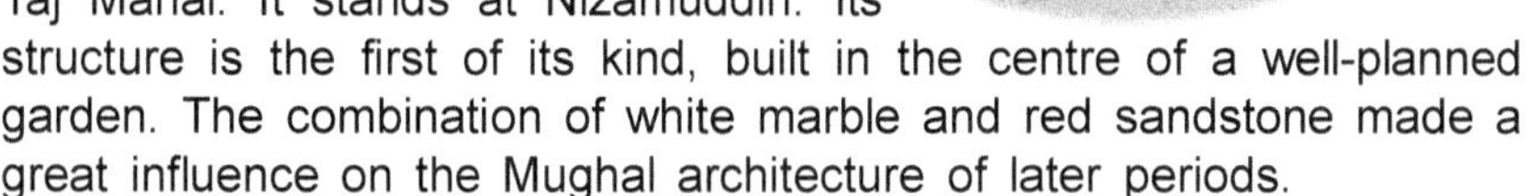 structure is the first of its kind, built in the centre of a well-planned garden. The combination of white marble and red sandstone made a great influence on the Mughal architecture of later periods.

LODI'S TOMBS

The Lodi tomb, mosques and monuments enclosed within the Lodi Gardens from a part of the remains of the city, which built by the Lodis. The tomb of Sikandar Lodi is located on the southernmost side of the Lodi Gardens. It was built in 1517-18. Due to limited financial means, the architecture of that period is prosaic, simple, austere and formal. Ordinary stone has been used in contrast to the marble or red stone, which was used with much delight by the Mughals.

LAL KOT

The first city of Delhi, the Lal Kot was built in around 1060 AD by the Hindu Tomar king, Anangpal. It was enlarged by Prithviraj Chauhan, the celebrated Rajput king. Except the walls on the western side of the fort, it has become a group of ruins. There are eight towers in the Lal Kot, the remains of which, are quite visible.

CHANDNI CHOWK

It is the nerve centre and a very busy commercial centre. In its ancient narrow lanes is still alive, traditional workmanship which makes Delhi famous. The main street of Old Delhi is a magnificent bazaar and as fine an example of congestion, colour and chaos as one finds in India today. During Shahjahan's reign, it was endowed with fine mansions and to had a tree-lined canal flowing to its centre. But today, it is jam-packed with artisans, traders and auto-rickshaws and comprises a fantastic cocktail of stench, movement, uproar and fumes. There is a

Jain temple at the street's eastern end, near the Red Fort; at the western end there is the Fatehpuri mosque.

FATEHPURI MOSQUE

Located at the western end of the Chandni Chowk, it is built of red sandstone and paved with black and white marble tiles. This mosque was constructed in 1650 by Fatehpuri Begum, one of the wives of the Mughal emperor, Shahjehan. There is a spacious courtyard as well as a fountain in its centre.

TOMB OF ILTUTMISH

The tomb, said to be the oldest tomb existing in India, was constructed by Raziya Sultana, the daughter of king Iltutmish. It is an example of Hindu art and design applied to a Muslim construction. It was built with red sandstone and marble and completed in 1236. Marble was used only in the central *mehrab* and cenotaph in the middle of the tomb's chamber. The identification of this tomb as that of Iltutmish is rather a controversial issue.

YOGMAYA TEMPLE

This temple stands at a distance of 250 yards from the Qutub Minar. From the study of the *Bhagwat Purana,* one comes to know that Yogmaya was the sister of Lord Krishana, The present temple is situated at the same spot where a temple built by Maharaja Yudhishthira was during the era of Mahabharata. The present temple was constructed by Lala Sidhoomal in 1827 A.D. The area of the temple is 400 square feet and its height is 42 feet. Inside the temple, there are two beautiful fans and in between the fans, the idol of the goddess has been placed.

TUGHLAK FORT

It is at a distance of 12 miles from of Old Delhi due its south. It was a massive stronghold built by Ghiasuddin Tughlak on a rock in 1324. The ranges of towers and bastions rendered the fort practically impregnable to an attack by any military method practised during those times. The fort has 13 gateways, 7 tanks and a remarkable well, which is 80 ft. deep and in the solid rocks. The defence of the fort consisted of walls rising above the rocks to a height of 40 ft, a 7-feet parapet and then, another 11 ft. of wall.

MASJID MOTH

A monument of the Sultanate period, it is perhaps the finest example of Lodi architecture in Delhi. Rising from a raised platform, the mosque is entered into from an elegant sandstone gateway in the east. The red sandstone is set off by bands of white marble with inscribed verses. Pierced by five openings, its central opening is built with red sandstone, ornamented with white marble and has a small window above its arch. The central *mehrab* in the prayer chamber is ornamented with Quranic inscriptions. The roof has three domes, rising from the central and end bays.

Other historical places of interest in Delhi are — Sultan Ghori's Tomb, Balban's Tomb, Bhim's Chhatank, Mughal Sarai, Rai Pithora Kot, Tomb and Mosque of Isa Khan, Sher Shah Mosque, Delhi Gate, Ghiyasuddin Tughlak's Tomb, Chaunsath Khamba, Old Idgah, Begumpuri Masjid, Agrasen ki Baoli, Quwwatul Islam Mosque, Tomb of Imam Zamin, Tomb of Iltutmish, Alauddin's Madrasa, Tomb of Kamali and Jamali and finally, Adam Khan's Tomb and Baoli, Hauz Khas.

▌ MODERN MONUMENTS ▌

INDIA GATE

It is a majestic high arch, 42 meters in terms of height. It was built as a memorial to about 90000 Indian soldiers who were killed during World War I. It was designed by Lutyens and took 10 years to complete. In 1972, amid celebrations of the Silver Jubilee of India's independence, a war memorial to the immortal soldiers was raised here. This simple monument has a helmet on the butt of a rifle, which is surrounded by four eternal flames (*Amar Jawan Jyoti*). From the base of the arch, one can get a  good view of the Rashtrapati Bhavan. A popular picnic spot, it accomodates hordes of people move about in the area and also on its lawns in summer evenings.

PARLIAMENT HOUSE

The Parliament House, also known as Sansad Bhawan, is a circular colonnade building, 171 m in terms of diameter and 75 ft. in terms of height. It comprises both the Houses of the Indian Parliament—the Lok

Sabha and the Rajya Sabha. It was in this building that the Constituent Assembly sat for three years to prepare the constitution of free India. It was designed by Sir Herbert Baker. Its foundation stone was laid in 1921. It was opened in 1927. Built on three levels, it has a storay of red sandstone foundation, a

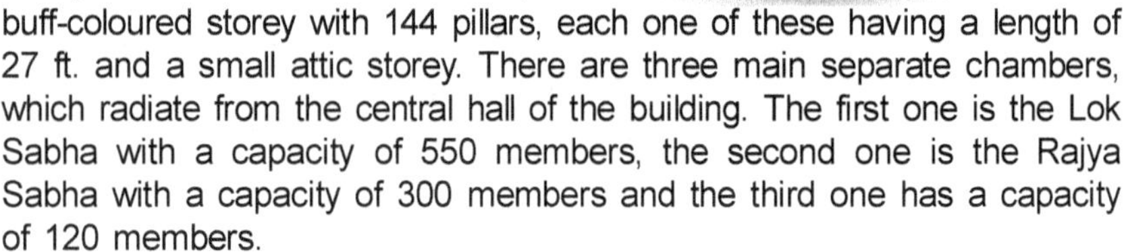

buff-coloured storey with 144 pillars, each one of these having a length of 27 ft. and a small attic storey. There are three main separate chambers, which radiate from the central hall of the building. The first one is the Lok Sabha with a capacity of 550 members, the second one is the Rajya Sabha with a capacity of 300 members and the third one has a capacity of 120 members.

RASHTRAPATI BHAVAN

It is the residence of the former Viceroy of India and presently, the residence of the President of India. It is renowned for its imperial design. This palace has 340 splendidly decorated rooms on the Raisina hill. Designed by Sir Edwin Lutyens, it was completed and occupied in 1929. It has an elegant Mughal Garden. The Durbar Hall (Audience Chamber), with its massive dome of a diameter of eight metres, golden pillars, white marble walls and flooring and a stone sculpture of standing Buddha, is used for formal ceremonies. Built of red and white sandstone, it stands on an estate having a total area of 330 acres and containing 12½ miles of corridors, 227 columns, 35 lobbies, 37 fountains.

THE SECRETARIAT

The secretariat building adjoining the Rashtrapati Bhavan was completed in 1930. Designed by Sir Herbert Baker, it consists of two blocks — North and South. Each block is surrounded by a dome, which is 217 ft. high. In the building, architecture has combined the best features of the English School of Architecture and the delicate traditional Indian architectural forms. It is possibly the greatest state office building in the world. The building consists of about 1000 rooms and approximately 8 miles of corridors. The interior decoration of the Secretariat is no less imposing than its splendid exterior. The North Block contains some beautiful and interesting paintings, which depict knowledge, justice, war and peace, spirits of the age, dances and music. The South Block contains the paintings related to holy and sacred cities of every religion and the emblems of old kings.

TEEN MURTI

This landmark sculpture in stone and bronze was created by Leonard Jenning in 1922. He was asked to prepare a statue that — should commemorate the martyrs of cavalry and armoured regiments of the Indian Army. Hence, these three handsome statues, denoting the soldiers from three Indian States — Hyderabad, Mysore and Jodhpur — were cast and collectively named Teen Murti. This statue was later installed in front of Commander in Chief's house, which became Jawaharlal Nehru's residence as the first Prime Minister of India. However, after his death, this building was converted into the Nehru Memorial Museum.

MARTYRS' MEMORIAL

The eminent sculptor, D. P. Roy Chowdhry, was commissioned to make a sculpture to depict the mood and spirit of the freedom struggle, which was led by Mahatma Gandhi. As it was not possible to show thousands of freedom fighters, it was decided to narrow them down to a team of eleven national heroes covering the vast cross-section of Indian society. This magnificent statue is 26 m. long and 3 m. high. It is cast in bronze. Thus, a unique sculptor, was created that fascinated the visitor's with its unique structure and message. It took 6 years to make it. Installed at the junction, where Sardar Patel Marg meets Willingdon Crescent, it is a popular spot for tourists.

NATIONAL WAR MEMORIAL

Nearly six decades after it was first proposed, Prime Minister Narendra Modi on February 25, 2019 inaugurated the National War Memorial, sprawled over 40 acres at the India Gate complex in the heart of the national capital. The Memorial has five concentric circles, named Rakshak Chakra, Amar Chakra, Veerta Chakra, Tyag Chakra, Param Yodha Sthal a central stone obelisk, and an eternal flame. The centre of the complex lies at a lower level than the surrounding features. The Memorial has been built at a cost of ₹ 176 crore.

CREMATION SITES OF NATIONAL LEADERS

On the banks of the river Yamuna, are the cremation sites of India's national leaders : (the place is followed by the name of the leader, in parentneses, who was cremated there) : Raj Ghat (Mahatma Gandhi), Shanti Vana (Jawaharlal Nehru), Vijay Ghat (Lal Bahadur Shastri), Shakti

Sthal (Indira Gandhi), Vir Bhumi (Rajiv Gandhi), Samata Sthal (Jagjivan Ram), Kisan Ghat (Charan Singh), Ekta Sthal (Giani Zail Singh) and Sadaiv Atal (Atal Behari Vajpayee). Raj Ghat, not far from the banks of the Yamuna river, has a simple black marble memorial to Mahatma Gandhi, marking the spot where he was cremated, following his assassination in 1948. Two museums dedicated to Gandhi are located nearby.

MEMORIALS TO NATIONAL HEROES

The Gandhi Museum, near Raj Ghat, houses many personal effects of Gandhiji and photographs depicting his life story. The memorial at Teen Murti House is a similar memorial to Jawaharlal Nehru. The Indira Gandhi Memorial is located at 1, Safdarjung Road, where she was assassinated.

▮ GARDENS ▮

Lodi Gardens: These gardens are in their full glory from January to March every year and can be approached from Lodi road and Max Muller Marg.

Mughal Gardens: Their gardens in Rashtrapati Bhavan are open to the public during the spring season for a fortnight only.

Rose Garden: This beautiful garden is situated at Shanti Path and contains several varities of roses.

Buddha Jayanti Park: It was established to commemorate the 2500th birth anniversary of Lord Buddha. It can be approached from the Ridge road, Sardar Patel Road or Shankar Marg.

Mahavira Garden: Situated on the ridge, it is dedicated to the Jain Tirthankar, Lord Mahavira.

Ajmal Khan Park: Spread over five acres in Karol bagh, it is popular for its musical fountain.

Talkatora Garden: Situated at Willingdon Crescent, it derives its name from the tank (*tal*) situated in it.

Nehru Park: It is an 85-acre landscaped garden in Chanakya Puri.

India Gate Lawns: These are known for lush green trees, which line Vijay Path and green lawns.

Children's Park: Near India Gate, it has swings, and an aquarium slides and is popular among children.

Zoological Garden: Situated between Purana Qila and Humayun's tomb, it has a number of species of animals, birds and aquatic creatures. It is also popularly called *Chidiya Ghar.*

Kalkaji District Park: Located near Nehru Place, it has lakes and terraced gardens.

Idgah: Green lawns surround the Idgah within the Hauz Khas enclave.

Dhaula Kuan Complex: This complex comprises an artificial lake, hanging bridge, waterfalls and a playground.

Deer Park: Located near Hauz Khas, this green area has a number of deer, rabbits and cranes. It can be approached from Hauz Khas village, Safdarjung Enclave or near the Delhi Lawn Tennis Association (DLTA) courts side.

District Park: It is a large green area with a pond full of ducks. It is located on the outer ring road, near Paschim Vihar.

Shalimar Bagh: This garden lies on the fringes of the city about 10 kms. due north-west of Old Delhi and is one of the most important Moghul gardens in the city. The beautiful central pavilion, the Shish Mahal, was built by Shahjahan. Although it is in a fairly advanced state of decay, yet some of the original painted flower decorations have survived.

Kalindi Kunj: Fountains, lit up with colourful lights at night, are its main attraction. It is located in South Delhi, near Badarpur.

NDMC Lake Park: It extends from the Safdarjung Flyover to Brigadier Hoshiar Singh road.

Okhla Dam: It is a good picnic spot near the Yamuna canal, and has fishing facilities as well.

Jahanpanah: It is a developed forest and tourists' delight in Chiragh Delhi.

Ladakh Buddha Vihar: It is situated near the ISBT on the Ring Road.

Yamuna Water Front: Boulevards, stretching up to 4 kms, with floral flocks and sprawling green lawns, are situated due south of Rajghat on this front.

▮ MUSEUMS AND ART GALLERIES ▮

History is brought to life, co-ordinating artistic excellence with scientific precision-Museums in Delhi represent an unmatched blend of the past with the present.

PARLIAMENT MUSEUM

This state-of-the-art museum exhibits the continuity of democratic heritage in India. The events are explained through a sound and light show alongwith the multimedia showcasing the period pictures and live mannequins. There is also a resource centre which has the data and pictures of those period. The museum has various sections includes Old Heritage depicting Buddha's conference, Din-e-Elahi; Independence movement displaying live pictures of Dandi March etc.; Transferring of kingdom; Bringing up of constitution; Works of Parliament; Parliament and World; Information Bank. Prior permission is required before visiting.

GANDHI NATIONAL MUSEUM

The museum has on display a few personal belongings of Gandhiji, who was a man of few things. A stone bowl and a brass plate, the clothes Gandhiji had worn on the day he was assassinated, a pair of wooden sandals, his walking bamboo stick, a few reed pens he carved himself and a diary in his own handwriting are the few interesting items on display. There is a library and an information centre in the same complex.

THE CHALLO DILLI MUSEUM, AZAD HIND GRAM

A treasure house of information, the museum houses visual reference and memorabilia, including original ranks and insignia associated with INA. The museum is in the memory of Subhash Chandra Bose, a freedom fighter who formed Azad Hind Fauj. An audio-visual facility adjoins the museum.

NEHRU MUSEUM

The residence of Pt. Jawahar Lal Nehru, the first Indian Prime Minister, Teen Murti Bhavan has been converted into a museum. The drawing-room & bedrooms are originally preserved and his personal belongings like gifts, photographs & awards are worth viewing.

NEHRU PLANETARIUM

The planetarium holds film shows on the solar system in English (11:30 am & 3:00 pm) and Hindi (1:30 & 4.00 pm). A special show in Hindi (10:30 am) is held on Sundays.

CRAFTS MUSEUM

With a collection of about 22000 objects, it provides a fascinating experience of traditional Indian crafts in textile, metal, wood and ceramic. This museum is worth visiting. It is located in the Pragati Maidan Exhibition Grounds, Mathura Road. It's part of a 'village life' complex where you can visit rural with the artisans working at their stalls. Admission is free.

NATIONAL SCIENCE CENTRE

Constructed in 8 floors this museum has working science exhibition as well as exhibits on the history of architecture. It has various sections for all age groups such as Heritage & Dinosaur gallery, Human Biology gallery, Fun Science Library etc. There are also a number of hands-on displays explaining the laws of physics. The Cyberlkool of this museum is the first fun-packed multimedia centre in the country. At least a whole day is required to go through this children's paradise.

NATIONAL MUSEUM

The Museum has a vast collection of Indian bronzes, terracotta (2700 BC) and wood sculptures dating back to the Maurya period (2nd-3rd century BC), various exhibits from the Vijayanagar period in south India, Mughal period, Indus Valley civilization, Greek-influenced Gandhara period and Gupta period.  Miniatures and mural paintings, costumes, arts and artefacts of various tribal people and precious jewellery heavily decorated with huge emeralds, diamonds and pearls from 2500 BC, famous bronze dancing statue from Mohenjodaro, wonderful collection of weapons, musical instruments, central Buddhist antiques and the autographed memories of the Mughal Emperor Jahangir are the eye-catchers at this museum. The rich and varied collection is spread over three spacious floors and at least one full day is required to see all the objects on display.

SHANKAR'S INTERNATIONAL DOLLS MUSEUM

A veritable dreamland for the children. 6000 dolls from 85 countries are on display at this museum in Nehru House at Bahadur Shah Zafar Marg. The India exhibit section comprises 500 dolls dressed in costumes worn from all over the country.

NATIONAL RAIL MUSEUM

This unique museum has a fascinating and exotic collection of over 100 real size exhibits of Indian Railways. Static and working models, signaling equipments, antique furnitures, historical photographs and related literature etc. are displayed in the museum. The line-up of old coaches includes the handsome Prince of Wales Saloon, built in 1875. Not to be outdone is the Maharaja of Mysore's Saloon built in 1899 with its brocade covered chairs and an elegant rosewood bed; one can peer in through the windows for a good look. A star attraction is the Fairy Queen, born in 1855 and considered to be one of the best preserved steam locomotive engines of her age. A ride in joy train and mono rail (PSMT) is the most exciting experience besides boating.

NATIONAL MUSEUM OF NATURAL HISTORY

An institution devoted to environmental education opened in 1978. Displaying a life size model of dinosaur in front of the museum and having three galleries inside it. The museum introduces the visitors with natural history, ecology and environment with plenty of examples from nature and various aspects of conservation of forest, wildlife, land, water and air. This museum also has a large collection of stuffed animals and birds.

MUSICAL INSTRUMENTS GALLERY

The gallery of musical instruments, a permanent exhibition, was opened in 1964 by Lord Yehudi Menuhin. This museum has a collection of about 600 musical instruments from all parts of the country.

INDIRA GANDHI SMRITI

Smt. Indira Gandhi's residence converted into a memorial after her assassination. There a large display of photographs on Indira Gandhi & her son Rajeev Gandhi can be seen. Some of Rajiv Gandhi's personal belongings are on display including the blasted and burnt clothing, taken off his blown up body, after he died during a bomb attack.

SANSKRITI MUSEUM

Consisting of two private museums-Museum of Everyday Art, with a unique collection of over 2000 objects, showing excellence in craftsmanship and conceptual innovation and Museum of Indian Terracotta displaying a collection of more than 1500 objects from witch living tradition of terracotta art in Indian regions.

TIBET HOUSE

This small museum has a fascinating collection of ceremonial items brought out of Tibet when the Dalai Lama fled following the Chinese occupation. There is a shop selling a wide range of Tibetan handicrafts. Lecture/discussion sessions are held regularly. The museum is open from Admission is free.

OLD FORT MUSEUM

Opened for general public on 22nd February, 2005, this museum is located inside the Old Fort. In it many interesting objects and fact sheets have been put on display including prehistoric tools that were found back to the Maurya period (300BC-200BC), Sunga period (200BC-100BC) and Saka-Kushan period (100BC-300AD) and finds a pride of place with Gupta period objects. The museum has details of the Old Fort, one of the oldest sites of Delhi, in particular and Delhi in general.

SRINIVAS MALLIAH MEMORIAL THEATRE CRAFTS AND MUSEUM

This small but unique museum houses a rare collection of traditional Indian theatre crafts including costumes, ornaments, headgear, carved images, effigies, musical instruments & handcrafted accessories with a large collection of traditional Indian puppets forms and carved wooden Bhuta and masks.

NATIONAL PHILATELY MUSEUM

Situated near Connaught Place, is Dak Bhawan which has a post office with an outlet for philatelists interested in Indian stamps. The building also houses the National Philatelic Museum which has an extensive stamp collection including the first stamp issued in India by the Sindh Dak (1854) and stamps issued before Independence by the rulers of the Princely States. Free entry passes from Parliament Street Head Post office basement.

RED FORT-SWATANTRATA SANGRAM SANGHRAHALYA

A definite stop for all those who wish to know more about the sweat, toil and blood that went into India's struggle for Independence. The museum is 100m beyond a left turn after Chatta Chowk near the Red Fort in Old Delhi. It traces India's history from the colonial period and focuses on the freedom movement and its leading lights. A comprehensive collection of photographs, paintings, maps, and bronzes makes for an interesting and educative experience. This is an excellent way to tell your kids about their country and the price our forefathers have paid for the freedom we enjoy today.

RED FORT-MUSEUM FOR ARCHAEOLOGY

Also known as Mumtaz Mahal Museum showcasing the precious objects and jewelleries of her age.

RED FORT-INDIAN WAR MEMORIAL MUSEUM

Above the Naubat Khana in Red Fort, this museum has weapons used in the First World War and some arms from Mughal Period.

DR AMBEDKAR NATIONAL MEMORIAL AND MUSEUM

This memorial is opened for general public on 6 December, 2003. There are two galleries exhibiting the photographs and articles, associated with Dr. Ambedkar and his activities during his life time, in the form of 100 displays alongwith literature and collected works (25 volumes).

AIR FORCE MUSEUM

Photographs from early days at Risalpur (now in Pakistan) & pioneers of World War I and II, Crests of various Squadrons and Commands, captured small arms during war of 1965 & 1971, Indian Air Force uniforms, models of various spacecrafts, aircrafts, Air Defence equipments, missiles are the main display at this museum in its two gallery section and in the main hangar houses sixteen different types of aircrafts including Wapiti (the first aircraft to fly through Khyber Pass). A corner has been dedicated to the first Indian Air Chief, Air Marshal Subroto Mukherjee.

KITCHEN MUSEUM

Inside Rashtrapati Bhawan, there is Kitchen Museum, which has on display items used to cook, serve, dine on and those used for picnics. The main attraction of this museum is 'The Star of India' with crockery of various sizes and designs. The exhibit also include silver cutlery, cutlery sets in different material, kitchenware, glassware, coffee maker, fruit stands, silver dishes, bowls, labels, cocktail shakers, scissors, picnic boxes etc. Museum is open for visitors on Mondays, Wednesdays, Fridays and Saturdays from 11 am. Prior permission is required to visit the museum.

SUPREME COURT MUSEUM

Divided into two sections, first section deals with the evolutions and development of Judiciary in India and the second deals with the Federal Court and the Supreme Court. Also on display in first section are, history of Indian legal system from British period, the Harappan seals and the head of a priest, Ashokan edict and Nalanda Copper plate of 9th Century A.D. In the second gallery antique furnitures, souvenirs, ceremonial costumes & wigs and files relating to land-mark judgements delivered by Supreme Court are on display. The records of famous cases such as Mahatma Gandhi murder case and Indira Gandhi assassination case etc. are also on display. Entry Free & photography prohibited.

SULABH INTERNATIONAL MUSEUM OF TOILETS

The founder of Sulabh International Social Service Organisation Dr. Bindeshwar Pathak envisioned this one of the rare museums, which has a rare collection of facts, pictures and objects detailing the historic evolution of toilets from 2500 BC to date and provides a chronological account of developments relating to technology, toilet related social customs, toilet etiquettes, prevailing sanitary conditions and legislative efforts of the times.

MUSEUM OF FOLK AND TRIBAL ART

Also known as K.C. Aryan's Home of Folk Art, was founded in 1984 by renowned painter, sculpture, art historian and a pioneer-collector of folk and tribal art objects. This is the only museum of its kind with the collection of folk, tribal & neglected art in India. The collection contains folk and tribal bronze icons, folk paintings from all over India. A prior appointment is preferred to visit the museum.

GHALIB ACADEMY

Inaugurated in 1969 by Late Dr. Zakir Hussain, President of India, the museum has been established in memory of great Urdu poet Mirza Asadullah Khan Ghalib. The academy has a museum dedicated to Ghalib showcasing statue, photographs, books and important documents of his age. It also has an art gallery where paintings made by famous & eminent artists like Satish Gujral, M.F. Hussain and others are on display.

ZAKIR HUSSAIN MEMORIAL TRUST

An exhibition of photographs, souvenirs & memorabilia, acquired during Dr. Zakir Hussain's term as President of India.

❚ ART GALLERIES ❚

- AIFACS, Rafi Marg
- Art Ribbons Art Gallery, Basant Lok, Vasant Vihar

- Ajanta Art Gallery, ICCR, Azad Bhavan, IP Estate
- Akshara Theatre, Baba Kharak Singh Marg
- Art Heritage for Contemporary Art, Triveni Kala Sangam, Tansen Marg
- Art Shop, Jharokha, Hauz Khas Village
- Delhi Art Gallery, Hauz Khas Village
- Dhoomi Mal Art Centre, Connaught Place
- Dhoomi Mal Collectors' Gallery, Connaught Circus
- Dhoomi Mal Ravi Jain Open Air Gallery Connaught Circus
- Gallery Espace, Community Centre, Friends Colony
- Gallery Ganesha, Greater Kailash Part II
- Gallery 42, Defence Colony
- Gallery Romain Rolland, Alliance Francaise, NDSE -II
- Gallery Steps, Suneja Chamber, Alaknanda
- Ladakh Art Gallery, Sunder Nagar Market
- La Divine, Lajpat Nagar-II
- Lalit Kala Akademi, Rabindra Bhavan
- Shahjahan Art Gallery, Basant Lok, Vasant Vihar
- Sculpture Garden, Connaught Circus
- Studio 55, Sunder Nagar
- Swastika Gallery & Sculpture Court, New Friends Colony
- Twinkle Art Gallery, Khan Market
- Vadhera Art Gallery, Defence Colony

▌CULTURAL CENTRES ▌

- Alliance Francaise Delhi, NDSE Part II
- American Centre, Kasturba Gandhi Marg
- Australia - India Council (AIC), Shantipath
- British Council Division, Kasturba Gandhi Marg
- Chamber Theatre, Triveni Kala Sangam, Tansen Marg
- Delhi Music Society, Nyaya Marg, Chanakyapuri
- Dilli Haat, INA Market

- Hungarian Cultural Centre, Janpath
- India Habitat Centre, Lodi Road
- Indian Council for Cultural Relations, Azad Bhavan, IP Estate
- India International Centre, Lodi Estate
- Indira Gandhi National Centre for Arts, Janpath
- Iran Culture House, Tilak Marg
- Italian Cultural Centre, Chandragupta Marg
- ITPO, Pragati Maidan
- Japan Cultural Centre, Feroze Shah Road
- Kathak Kendra, Bhagwan Das Road
- Lalit Kala Akademi, Feroze Shah Road, Rabindra Bhavan
- Max Mueller Bhavan, Kasturba Gandhi Marg
- National School of Drama, Bahawalpur House
- NSD Repertory Company, Rabindra Bhavan
- Portuguese Cultural Centre, Sunder Nagar
- Russian Science & Culture Centre, Feroze Shah Road
- Sahitya Akademi, Rabindra Bhavan
- Sahitya Kala Parishad, Satsang Vihar Marg
- Sangeet Natak Akademi, Rabindra Bhavan
- Shriram Bharatiya Kala Kendra, Copernicus Marg

▌ AUDITORIA ▌

- Air Force Auditorium, Subroto Park
- Aiwan-e-Ghalib Auditorium, Mata Sundari Lane
- Ambedkar Auditorium, Ashoka Road
- Falaknuma & Hamsadhwani Theatres, Pragati Maidan
- FICCI Golden Jubilee Auditorium, Tansen Marg
- Gandhi Memorial Hall, Bahadur Shah Zafar Marg
- India International Centre, Lodi Estate
- Jawaharlal Nehru Auditorium, AIIMS
- Kamani Auditorium, Copernicus Marg
- LTG Auditorium, Copernicus Marg

- Mavalankar Auditorium, Rafi Marg
- Pirojsha Godrej National Conservation Centre, Lodi Estate
- Rabindra Rangshala, Upper Ridge Road
- Sapru House, Barakhamba Road
- Siri Fort Auditorium, Asiad Village
- Shri Ram Centre, Safdar Hashmi Road
- Tagore Hall, ICCR, Azad Bhavan
- Talkatora Indoor Stadium, Talkatora Road
- Teen Murti Auditorium, Teen Murti House.
- Triveni Kala Sangam, Tansen Marg
- Vigyan Bhavan, Maulana Azad Road

▋ CINEMA HALLS ▋

Delhi have a lot of movie hall be it a single screen theaters or a swanky multiplexes. Following is the list best known movies theaters in and around Delhi.

Fun Cinemas	PVR	Satyam	Wave Cinemas
Motinagar	EDM	Patel Nagar	Raja Garden
Pitampura	Saket	Janak Place	
Cross River Mall	Priya	Nehru Place	
V3S	Rivoli		
	Naraina		
	Vikaspuri		
	Prashant Vihar		

▋ SCIENCE CENTERS ▋

- Nehru Planetarium, Teen Murti House
- National Science Centre, Bhairon Road
- National Zoological Park, Mathura Road

▋ SPORTS STADIA ▋

Delhi has a good infrastructure for organizing sports activities. Most of the stadia were built for organising the IX Asian Games, which were held in New Delhi in 1982. The best known stadia are: **Jawaharlal Nehru Stadium** (for Athletics and football) with a seating capacity of 75,000; **Indira Gandhi Indoor Stadium** (for gymnastics, table tennis, basketball, badminton and having a seating capacity of 25000 persons); **Yamuna Velodrome** and having a seating capacity of 2250 persons); **Talkatora Indoor Stadium** (for swimming and table tennis); **Shivaji Stadium** (for hockey); **Ferozeshah Kotla** (for cricket); **National Stadium** (for hockey); **R K Khanna Lawn tennis Stadium** and the **Tughlakabad Shooting Range**. Besides these, facilities for other games are also available. Delhi Tourism & Transportation Development Corporation organises adventure activities on special demand in Delhi as well as in the nearby areas. Rock climbing is organised at Lado Sarai near Qutab Minar. Para-Sailing is done on special demand at Dhauj in Haryana.

▎ PLACES OF WORSHIP ▎

BIRLA MANDIR

The famous temple is known as Laxmi Narayan Mandir and is dedicated to Lord Vishnu. Structurally similar to old temples of Orissa, the chief temple houses the marble idols of Lord Vishnu and Goddess Laxmi. On its either side, are installed the idols of Goddess Durga and Lord Shiva in separate temples. It was built by Raja Baldev Das Birla in 1938. Adjacent to the same, on one side, is Gita Bhavan, containing a grand and attractive statue of, Lord Krishna and the beautiful paintings from *the Mahabharta*. On the other side of the central structure, is an excellent temple of the Lord Buddha. There are also wall paintings related to his life and teachings. On the walls and in upper gallery, there are numerous wonderful paintings and epitomes of all the great teachings of Hinduism.

CHHATTARPUR TEMPLE

This complex near Mehrauli has a small temple devoted to the Goddess Kali and was constructed 50 years ago. There are shrines devoted to the gods and goddesses of the Hindu pantheon. The Hanuman temple has *Hanuman Chalisa* and *Hanuman Aarti* inscribed on either side of the wall. There is a beautifully carved metal door in the Sita Ram temple. Next to this temple, is the Mata Mandir. The foyer has lions and nymphs cast in bronze. The walls of the hall

are adorned with paintings of several Hindu goddesses and portraits of important spiritual leaders. The first thing one sees after entering into the temple complex is a huge pipul tree decked with colourful knotted handkerchiefs tied to its branches. The common belief among devotees is that this wishing tree has magical powers and can fulfil their desires.

KALKAJI MANDIR

Located due South-east of Nehru Place and adjacent to Kalkaji, this temple is dedicated to Goddess Kali. According to a tradition, this temple stands on the site of a temple built as early as 3000 B.C. The oldest part of the present temple was built in 1764. The idol of Goddess Kali is placed in the centre of this temple and is completely covered with brocade and red cloth. It is enclosed on three sides by red sandstone and white marble railing.

DIGAMBER JAIN TEMPLE

This is one of the innumerable Jain temples in Delhi. However, it is the oldest and the most impressive one. It is situated opposite Red Fort. In the main shrine, Lord Parasnath's image is installed. This temple was built in 1526. The chief image is placed on the central altar. The interior of the complex is profusely painted and carved.

JAIN TEMPLE, DHARAM PURA

Built in 1810, this temple is considered an architectural gem of highest purity in which, both the mosaic and inlaid craft foems have retained their loftiest perfection. The *kamal* on which, the image of Shri Adi Nath Bhagvan was completed, is unique. In 1938, a repair programme was executed on all the old paintings in the dome and the walls were painted afresh.

HANUMAN MANDIR

A popular religious spot, the Hanuman Mandir is situated near Connaught Circus. It was built most probably at the same time when the Jantar Mantar was built. From an architectural viewpoint, it is quite significant. It is mostly frequented on Tuesdays, the day dedicated especially to Hanuman.

SRI SRI RADHA PARTHASARATHI TEMPLE

The temple stands at Hari Krishna Hill, Sant Nagar, near East of Kailash. This magnificent temple has *shikhars* of a height of 90 ft. above the ground level. There are beautiful paintings of Russian artists on different aspects of the life of Radha Krishna, Sita, Ram, Laxman, Hanuman and Chaitanya Mahaprabhu. Along with the temple, a centre, known as the Glory of India's Vedic Culture.

SHIVA'S STATUE

On the National Highway No. 8, a grand statue of Lord Shiva has been erected. This wonderful 65-foot tall statue, built with reinforced cement concrete, has been finished in copper and was installed in 1994.

THE LOTUS TEMPLE

The design of this Baha'i House of Worship was inspired by the lotus, the exquisitely beautiful flower and symbol of purity, which is associated with devotion in India. It is a temple of pin drop silence. Located close to Nehru Place, on a hill, this gleaming lotus-shaped structure in white is one of the most visited monuments of Delhi. A pathway through the middle of finely maintained lawns leads to this 27-petal edifice surrounded by 9 large pools of water. Inside the prayer hall, all are welcome to meditate and pray in silence. There are teachings of the Baha'i faith inscribed on wall-hung panels. The prayer hall is naturally lit through the well designed alignment of the petals and naturally cooled.

GURUDWARA BANGLA SAHIB

Near the Gol Dakkhana roundabout, is the Gurudwara Bangla Sahib, which is conspicuous from the road side by its gold-leaf domes. As the story goes, the eighth sikh Guru, Harkishan Sahib, stayed in a bungalow situated here. Guruji had also got a lake dug in this complex. The waters of this lake are attributed with medicinal effects and there is always a rush to take it home.

GURUDWARA RAKABGANJ

It is a famous imposing Sikh shrine situated at the corner of Church road and Pandit Pant Marg. This is the place where the beheaded body of the ninth Guru of Sikhs, Guru Tegh Bahadur, was cremated in 1675.

GURUDWARA SIS GANJ

Gurudwara Sis Ganj is one of the shrines most revered by the Sikh community. It is in Chandni Chowk. As the story goes, Guru Tegh Bahadur was beheaded here on November 11, 1675 under the orders of emperor Aurangzeb. Gurudwara Sis Ganj stands on the site of the martyrdom of the Guru. Sprinklers at the base of the first step wash people's feet as they start moving upwards in the shrine. The trunk of the tree under which, the Guru attained martyrdom, is still preserved in one corner of the hall of this gurudwara.

SACRED HEART CATHEDRAL

It is a popular Catholic Church, situated opposite the Gol Dakkhana. It has been constructed on a long rectangular plot with its axis running from north to south. The construction of the Cathedral was completed 1934.

FREE CHURCH

Situated near Jantar Mantar, this main church building is surmounted by triangular pediments on all sides. The doorways have conical canopies resting on white-painted columns. The centre of the hall has a raised conical dome. The colour scheme of red plaster, relieved with white bands and state roofs, is very appealing. The reason for its immense popularity lies in the fact that people can worship here freely without any denominational constraints.

DARGAH QUTAB SAHIB

It is located near Qutab Minar. Emperor Iltutmish had got it constructed. Hazrat Qutubuddin Bakhtiar Kaki was a well-known Sheikh but after arriving in India, he became a disciple and later, the spiritual successor of Hazrat Khwaja Moinuddin Chishti of Ajmer. Close to his shrine, are several halls, mosques and tanks.

DARGAH HAZRAT NIZAMUDDIN AULIA

Hazrat Nizamuddin Aulia was a saint of great repute who passed away in 1325. This Dargah is a resting place of some famous persons, namely, Hazrat Amir Khusrou, Jahanara Begam (the daughter of Shahjehan), Agha Khan, Emperor Mohammed Shah and Mirza Ghalib. This Dargah is of religious importance and is visited by thousands of devout pilgrims not only from India, but also from other countries. It is regarded by the Muslims as one of the most sacred places of pilgrimage in India. This dargah is located in a posh colony of South Delhi, which is at a distance of nearly 5 kms. from ITO.

CHARAGH DILLI

The shrine of Hazrat Nasiruddin Roshan Chiragh, the spiritual heir of Hazrat Nizamuddin Aulia, is situated at Chiragh Dilli.

DARGAH SHEIKH SAHIB

The shrine of Hazrat Sheikh Kalimullah, a saint in the Chishti order, is situated opposite the Red Fort. It is situated just below, the Jama Masjid in Old Delhi.

▌ MAJOR MARKETS ▌

CONNAUGHT PLACE

Connaught Place is the foremost shopping centre of New Delhi, which has been built in a horse-shoe pattern. It comparises inner, middle and outer circles. It came up in 1931 with the official transfer of the Capital from Calcutta to Delhi. It has two concentric circles of colonial buildings with colonnaded verandahs surrounding the central park. The outer circle is called Connaught Circus while the inner circle is called Connaught Place. It is also an all types entertainment center with of road shows happening here every now and then. It also marks the distance of zero km to New Delhi. Its major attraction is the restaurants, book shops and art and craft shops. It is closed on Sundays.

KAROL BAGH

It is centrally located just 2 kms away from New Delhi Railway Station. This market, known for clothes, readymades, leather bags, gold jewellery and car accessories, developed after the partition. It is closed on Mondays.

CENTRAL MARKET, LAJPAT NAGAR

It is located in south-central Delhi, touching Ring Road. It sells the famous brands for all household items, including clothes and white goods. It has seen large expansion during recent times. It is closed on Mondays.

GANDHI NAGAR MARKET

It is located across the Yamuna river and is known for readymade garments, woollens and clothes. It is closed on Sundays.

SADAR BAZAR

It is the wholesale market of the city for buying almost anything. It is located close to both the major railway stations as well as the ISBT at Mori Gate. People from far off places of northern India visit the market frequently. It is closed on Sundays.

PALIKA BAZAR

It is located in the inner circle of Connaught Place. This market is known for bargains and one can get garments, electronic goods and foreign items from its shops. It is underground and air-conditioned. It is closed on Sundays.

JANPATH

It is famous for inexpensive *chappals* or sandals, leather bags, readymade garments, cosmetics, metal/brass art pieces and artificial jewellery. A cluster of a few shops are known as Tibetan market, where bronze and copper figures, paintings, antiques, semi-precious wares and quaint bangles, rings and other costume jewellery are sold. It is closed on Sundays.

SHANKAR MARKET/SUPER BAZAR

Adjacent to Connaught Place, Shankar Market offers readymade garments, tailoring services, leather goods, dry fruits etc. Next to it, is Super Bazaar which is a large departmental store with everything under its roof. It is closed on Sunday.

PANCHKUIAN ROAD

It is one of the best markets for furniture and household fittings. Lamp shades, decorative items brass and furniture are available here. It is located on the road leading to Connaught Place. It is closed on Sundays.

CHANDANI CHOWK

The main lane of old Delhi was laid out by emperor Shahjahan and was once, one of the major trading centers of Asia. Today, it is an attractive shopping center, with an old-world atmosphere. The jewellery center is located at Dariba Kalan, the largest ivory mart at Jama Masjid, exotic silk saries centre at Paranthe Wali Gali and Nai Sarak, books shops at Nai Sarak, crystalware and chandelier stores at Meena Bazar and finally, filigree and gold brocade shops at Kinari Bazar. Khari Baoli, the street that runs from the Fatehpuri Mosque to the western edge of the old city, is Delhi"s bustling wholesale spice market. It is closed on Sundays.

SOUTH EXTENSION I & II

These are one of the most modern markets of Delhi. The market of South Extension (Part II) in located on the side of Khel Gaon Marg. The market of South Extension (Part I) is located on the periphery of Kotla Mubarakpur. Both these markets have shops adjacent to Ring Road, though these have also peretcated the colonies of South Extension (part I and II) as well. Most of the reputed brand names of the world are found here. It is a nice for eating and shopping. It is closed on Mondays.

SAROJINI NAGAR MARKET

This market is a favourite of the middle class families. White goods, garments, electronic goods, various types of foods, toys, crockery and garments are available in this market. It is closed on Mondays.

HAUZ KHAS VILLAGE

This market has a harmonious blend of the Indian tradition and the contemporary style. Fashion designers have their own boutiques and retail outlets here. It also has a specialty restaurant complex and lots of good art galleries. It is closed on Tuesdays.

JWALA HERI

This market is the popular place of shopping for the residents of west Delhi. It even attracts people from nearby towns. It is closed on Wednesdays.

Administration   4

THE present system of administration in Delhi can be traced back to 1803, when Delhi had come under British protection; eventually, the city became a part of the British Punjab. The Delhi district had a Deputy Commissioner who was the Chief District Officer, having powers in the matters of revenue and Registration powers. He was also the head of urban administration as he was the President of the District Board and the Municipality.

Till independence, Delhi had a Chief Commissioner as its administrative and executive head, with the Deputy Commissioner reporting to him. He had three Assistant Commissioners to share responsibilities such as case work of revenue and criminal appeals, municipal and minor criminal cases and administration of the municipality.

SPECIAL STATUS FOR DELHI

After independence, Government of India, aware of the special status of Delhi and its problems, set up a committee, under the chairmanship of Dr. Pattabhi Sitaramayya to consider its future set-up. The Committee recommended that the Delhi province should be under a Lieutenant-Governor, appointed by the President and a Council of Ministers with a Chief Minister at the head to assist and advise the Lieutenant-Governor and responsible to the elected Provincial Legislature. There was a provision that any differences arising between the Lieutenant-Governor and the Ministry should be referred to the President a for final decision. The Drafting Committee of the constitution did not approve these recommendations. The Constituent Assembly left the entire matter regarding the administrative set-up of Part C States, including Delhi, to the Parliament.

DELHI'S FIRST ASSEMBLY

Under the States Act (Part 'C'), Delhi was provided with a Legislative Assembly and Council of Ministers to aid and advise the Chief

Commissioner from 1952; this pattern continued till 1956. However, Delhi did not have the power to make laws in regard to public order, police (including railway police), constitution and powers of the Municipal Corporation and other local authorities, improvement trust, water supply, drainage, electricity, transport and other public utility authorities of Delhi or New Delhi land and buildings vested in or in the possession of the union government. Despite these limitations, the authority of Delhi Assembly looked after administration of justice, prisons, public health, agriculture, industries etc. The union government also had the power to extend any enactment in force in Part A States with or without any modifications. However, this system of dual control or diarchy seemed to satisfy none.

CENTRALLY ADMINISTERED NATIONAL CAPITAL

In December 1953, the States Reorganisation Commission was set up. The Commission was of the opinion that the dual control arising from the division of responsibility between the central government and the state government had resulted in a marked deterioration of administrative standards in the city. Hence, the Commission opined that it should be under full control of the union government. The Government of India accepted the recommendations of the Commission and Delhi ceased to have a local legislature. It became a Union Territory in November, 1956. The Ministry of Home Affairs had the overall responsibility for the city and acted as a coordinating agency while such specific matters were dealt with by other ministries as were able and powerful to sort these out. Delhi's budget formed a part of the central budget and Parliament attended to its legislative needs.

DELHI ADMINISTRATION ACT

The aforementioned arrangement continued till 1966 when, due to persistent demands from the people of Delhi for a popular government, the Delhi Administration Act (1966) came into force. It provided for a Metropolitan Council. Under the new set-up, the Union Territory of Delhi remained the responsibility of the centre, in terms of law and reality. The President functioned as the Executive Head of the Union Territory with the Lieutenant Governor as his agent. Parliament was the sole authority to make laws on all the matters in respect of Delhi. The Union Ministry of Home Affairs had the overall responsibility and acted as a coordinating agency. Other ministries dealt with specific matters coming within their respective purviews. The Union Ministry of Agriculture dealt directly with the Delhi Milk Scheme, the Ministry of Surface Transport with the Delhi Transport Corporation and the Ministry of Urban Development with the Delhi Development Authority and so on.

METROPOLITAN COUNCIL

Under the Delhi Administration Act (1966), Delhi had a representative Assembly, called Metropolitan Council, whose role was essentially advisory, and also a small Executive Council, which functioned in strict subordination to the Lieutenant Governor and the President of India. The Metropolitan Council consisted of 56 members directly elected for a term of five years and not more than five members nominated by the central government. The Metropolitan Council was empowered to discuss and make recommendations with respect to proposals for undertaking legislations for Delhi, budget proposals, development schemes and administrative matters involving general policy, proposals for legislation or any other matter referred to it by the Lieutenant Governor from the State List or the Concurrent List. The resolutions of the Metropolitan Council, however, had no binding force. It was more or less a debating council.

EXECUTIVE COUNCIL

The Executive Council consisted of four members one of whom was designated as the Chief Executive Councillor. The   Executive Councillors were appointed by the President of India from   amongst the members of the Metropolitan Council and held their offices during his pleasure. The Executive Council and its members were not made responsible to the Metropolitan Council and had no accountability to the people of Delhi. Each Executive Councillor was assigned a group of departments and was made responsible for the disposal of the work of those departments. The Executive Council was required to assist and advise the Lieutenant Governor in the exercise of his functions and in respect of matters enumerated in the State List or the Concurrent List, except where he was required by law to act on his discretion. The advice of the Executive Council was not binding on the Lieutenant Governor.

RESERVED SUBJECTS

The reserved subjects included functions of judicial and quasi-judicial nature and law and order in Delhi, including the organisation and discipline of the police force. The reserved subjects also included various services, housing and land and building departments of the Delhi

Administration, which were kept out of the purview of the Cabinet. Similarly, the U.T. Government had no control over matters pertaining to the service personnel in the Delhi Government. The Chief Secretary, Finance Secretary, Development Commissioner, Commissioner of Police and other senior posts in the Delhi Government required the approval of the central government. Hence, the setting up of the Assembly and the NCT Government did not absolve the Government of India or Parliament of their constitutional responsibilities for the administration of Delhi.

GENERAL ADMINISTRATION

The guiding principle governing the relations of the central government with the Delhi Administration was that in respect of 'transferred' subjects, irrespective of the legal position, the central government must treat Delhi in a manner similar to any state government, particularly in matters of day-to-day administration. In regard to "reserved subjects", however, where the central government's responsibility could directly be related to the administration of the national capital, it had to take keen interest. There were reserved Departments dealing with all the service matters; Home (Police Department) dealing with Law and Order and Magistracy; Land and Building; and the Master Plan of Delhi. The 'transferred' departments included Home (General) Jails, Vigilance, Local Self-Government and Public Works Department, Law and Justice, Transport (including DTC), Agriculture and Irrigation, Animal Husbandry, Planning etc.

PRESENT FORM OF DELHI ASSEMBLY

The erstwhile Delhi Metropolitan Council set-up suffered from many inherent deficiencies. It was a deliberative organ with no legislative powers and it had only an advisory role in the governance of Delhi. There was, therefore, a continuous demand for a full fledged State Assembly with Council of Ministers to aid and advice the Lt. Governor. Accordingly, on 24th December 1987, the Government of India appointed the "Sarkaria Committee" (later on called "Balakrishnan Committee") to go into the various issues connected with the administration of Union Territory of Delhi and to recommend measures for streamlining the administrative set up. The Committee submitted its report on 14th December 1989.

In accordance with the recommendations of the Balakrishnan Committee, the Parliament passed the **Constitution (69th Amendment)**

Act, 1991, which inserted the new Articles 239 AA and 239 AB in the Constitution providing, inter alia, for a Legislative Assembly for Delhi. Another comprehensive legislation passed by Parliament called "The Government of National Capital Territory of Delhi Act, 1991", supplements the Constitutional provisions relating to the Legislative Assembly and the Council of Ministers and matters related thereto. Section 33 of the Government of National Capital Territory of Delhi Act provides for the framing of the Rules of Procedure and Conduct of Business of the Legislative Assembly.

The Assembly consists of 70 Members–all chosen by direct election from as many constituencies. At present 13 seats in the Assembly are reserved for Scheduled Castes. The Constitution lays down that the strength of the Council of Ministers shall not be more than ten per cent of the total number of members in the Assembly. Thus, there are Seven Ministers in the Delhi Cabinet.

The Assembly has the power to make laws with respect to all the matters in the State List or in the Concurrent List of the Constitution of India except Entries 1 (Public Order), 2 (Police), and 18 (Land), and entries 64, 65 and 66 relatable to the said entries of the State List.

The President appoints the Chief Minister and on the advice of the Chief Minister appoints other Ministers. The Ministers hold office during the pleasure of the President. The Chief Minister and her Council aids and advises the Lt. Governor in the exercise of his functions in relation to matters with respect to which the Legislative Assembly has power to make laws.

The Lieutenant Governor has the power to summon, prorogue or dissolve the Assembly. He can also address the Assembly or send messages to it. The Lt. Governor addresses the first session of the Assembly after each general elections and the first session of each year.

The Assembly is a privileged body and its members enjoy the freedom of speech in the House as well as freedom to vote. The Members of the Delhi Assembly have all the powers and privileges, which are enjoyed by the Members of Parliament. The proceedings of the Assembly cannot be called in question in the Court of Law. Also the Member or the Presiding Officer in whom powers are vested for regulating the procedure or conduct of business is not subject to the jurisdiction of Courts in respect of exercise by him of those powers.

Like members of other State Legislatures and Parliament, the members of Delhi Legislative Assembly are also empowered to vote in the election of the President of India. They are also subject to the Tenth Schedule of the Constitution, which contains provisions as to disqualification on grounds of defection.

The Present Assembly has certainly more powers than the Metropolitan Council and the one Delhi had in 1952 under the Part-C States Act, 1951. Now only 3 subjects are outside the purview of the Legislative Assembly, whereas as many as 9 subjects were outside the competence of the 1952 Assembly.

LIEUTENANT GOVERNOR

The Lieutenant Governor is the head of the government. There is a Council of Ministers to aid and advise him, while he performs his functions except when he is required to act in his discretion. The Lieutenant Governor shall act in his discretion in a matter; (i) which falls outside the purview of the powers conferred on the Legislative Assembly but in respect of which, the powers or functions are entrusted or delegated to him by the President; or (ii) in which, he is required by or under any law to act in his discretion or exercise any judicial or quasi-judicial functions. If any question arises as to whether any matter is or is not a matter with respect to which, the Lieutenant Governor is, by or under any law, required to act in his discretion, the decision of the Lieutenant Governor thereon shall be deemed final. It is the duty of the Chief Minister to: communicate to the Lieutenant Governor all the decisions of the Council of Ministers relating to the administration of the affairs of the capital and proposals for legislation; furnish such information relating to the administration of the affairs of the capital and proposals for legislation as Lieutenant Governor may call for ; and if the Lieutenant Governor so requires, submit, for the consideration of the Council of Ministers, any matter on which, a decision has been taken by a minister but it has not been considered by the Council.

The Lieutenant Governor is also an essential part of the Legislative Assembly as no Bill passed by the Legislative Assembly can become a law unless assented to by the Lieutenant Governor. The Lieutenant Governor can not give assent to and has to reserves for the consideration of the President, any Bill, which (a) in the opinion of the Lieutenant Governor, would, if it became a law, so derogate from the powers of the High Court as to endanger the position, which that Court is, according to the Constitution, designed to fill; or (b) the President may, by an order, direct to be reserved for his consideration, or any other matter specified under the law. When a Bill is reserved for the consideration of the President, the President shall declare either that he assents to the Bill or that he withholds his assent therefrom. The President may also issue a message for the consideration of the legislative assembly.

The remote control by the central government makes the position of the Lieutenant Governor much more difficult and unenviable when, directly or indirectly, the state of affairs comes under the discussion or review in the Legislative Assembly at the time of budget discussion of either the government or of the DDA. Thus, the Council of Ministers continuously presses for being consulted or at least, being kept informed.

LEGISLATIVE ASSEMBLY

The total number of seats in the Legislative Assembly to be filled by direct election from the territorial constituencies is seventy. Seats are reserved for the Scheduled Castes in the Legislative Assembly. The number of seats reserved is, as nearly as may be, in the same proportion to the total number of seats in the Assembly as the population of Scheduled Castes in the capital bears to the total population of the capital. The Assembly, unless dissolved sooner, continues for five years from the date appointed for its first meeting. The said period may, while a Proclamation of Emergency issued under Article 352 is in operation, be extended by the President, by his order, for a period not exceeding one year at a time and not extending in any case beyond a period for six months after such Proclamation has ceased to operate. The Lieutenant Governor summons the Legislative Assembly to meet at such time and place as he deems fit. But six months shall not intervene between its last sitting in one session and the date appointed for its first sitting in the next session. The Lieutenant Governor may prorogue or dissolve the Assembly at any point of time. The Legislative Assembly chooses two members of the Assembly to be Speaker and Deputy Speaker respectively. The assembly can remove either of them. Whenever the Assembly is dissolved, the Speaker shall not vacate his office until immediately before the first meeting of the Assembly after the dissolution. The Speaker or Deputy Speaker cannot preside while a resolution for his removal from his office is under consideration. The Lieutenant Governor may address the Legislative Assembly and for this purpose, is require the attendance of its members. The Lieutenant Governor may send messages to the Assembly either with respect to a Bill pending in the Assembly or otherwise.

FINANCIAL POWERS

The Delhi Government presents its budget in the Legislative Assembly for approval. No expenditure can be incurred without the approval of the Assembly; likewise, no tax can be imposed without its approval. The Bill for imposition, abolition, remission, alteration or regulation of any tax or appropriation of moneys out of the Consolidated Fund of the Capital is moved in the Legislative Assembly only on the recommendation of the Lieutenant Governor.

OTHER MATTERS OF DISCRETION

Apart from the subjects, expressly excluded from the purview of the Council of Ministers there are certain other matters in which, Lieutenant Governor is required to exercise his discretion or individual judgement and need not consult the Council of Ministers. For instance, the Governor has a right to appoint the Chief Minister in a state. Other ministers have to be appointed by the Governor on the advice of the Chief Minister. Before appointing a Chief Minister, the Governor has to make sure that he commands a majority in the Legislative Assembly of the state.

ADMINISTRATION

The NCT of Delhi continues to be a Union Territory and hence, it cannot have its own cadres of IAS and IPS officials. The Ministry of Home Affairs is the controlling authority for these cadres as well as that of DANICS and DANIPS and controls their postings and transfers. The administration of NCT of Delhi, which implements the decisions and policies of the government, consists of the Secretariat. It is headed by the Chief Secretary and comprises several Secretaries of the administrative departments, viz Home, Law, Finance, Planning, Food Supplies, Agriculture, Horticulture, Forestry, Wildlife, Animal Husbandry, Poultry, Fisheries, Rural Development, Irrigation, Flood Control, Agricultural Marketing, Energy Development, Cooperative Societies, Industries, Labour, Education, Delhi Archives, Archaeology, Social Welfare, Transport, Tourism, Health and Family Welfare. There are also some other offices that function under the Delhi Government, viz, Directorate of Transport and Tourism, Directorate of Employment and Training, Directorate of Information and Publicity, Public Works

Department, Directorate of Industries, Cooperative Societies Department, Bureau of Economics and Statistics, Directorate of Social Welfare, Sales Tax Commissioner etc. The administration of NCT of Delhi is carried on by civil servants, belonging to various cadres such as Indian Administrative Service (IAS), Indian Police Service (IPS), Delhi and Andaman Nicobar Island Civil Service (DANICS), Delhi and Andaman Nicobar Island Police Service (DANIPS) and others.

COORDINATION

The Delhi Government has to closely coordinate its activities and those of its local bodies like the Municipal Corporation of Delhi, New Delhi Municipal Council, Delhi Cantonment Board etc. as well as those agencies/corporations established by the central government, such as the Delhi Development Authority. In order to achieve the desired level of coordination, there is a Standing Committee, which is headed by the Chief Secretary and comprising Vice-chairman of the DDA, the Commissioner of the MCD, the Chairman of the DVB and the Administrator of the NDMC with the Secretary of the Local Self-government as its Member Secretary.

THE LOCAL BODIES

The following Local Bodies operate in the Union Territory of Delhi: the Municipal Corporation of Delhi; the New Delhi Municipal Council; and the Delhi Cantonment Board. Out of the capital's total area of 1483 sq. kms., the MCD occupies an area of 1398 sq. km. (94 per cent), whereas NDMC and Delhi Cantonment occupy the areas of 43 sq. kms (3 per cent) and 43 sq. km. (3 per cent), respectively. Delhi's 97% population lives in the areas under MCD's jurisdiction whereas 2% and 1% people live in NDMC and Delhi Cantonment areas, respectively.

MUNICIPAL CORPORATION
OF DELHI (MCD)

HISTORY OF MCD

The origin of civic administration in Delhi can be traced way back to the year 1862 when Delhi Municipal Commission came into existence. At that time, the city was confined to an area of two square miles with

1.21 lakh inhabitants. The infrastructure of civic services, set up by Shahjahan, the builder of the city, about 200 years prior to formation of the civic body, had even then, become out-moded and out-dated. The work had, therefore, to be started from a scratch. In 1863, the sanitation and conservancy system was set up and public latrines were constructed. A Unani dispensary was opened in Sadar Bazar and for the first time, registration of births and deaths was introduced. This nascent civic body took financial assistance from the government to fulfil its obligations, with fifty per cent being spent on the police establishment. Octroi revenues were the main source of income.

The Clock Tower and the Town Hall building were constructed in 1866 and the present building was reconstructed in 1947. A fire fighting system was introduced in 1867, with one fire engine stationed at Kotwali. As well water was not found fit for consumption, potable water was supplied by water carts in 1871-72. The proposal to set up a water works establishment was initiated in 1869. The first street lighting system was introduced in 1870 with lantern and lamp-posts. Electricity came much later but before the Durbar event in 1911. Primary education was started in 1857 by taking over existing schools and opening new ones. Although gardens and horticulture had occupied the attention of the administration from the very beginning, yet mass plantation of 1600 saplings was done in 1875. Later, the Delhi Municipal Commission was replaced by the Delhi Municipal Committee, which functioned as the only civic body for about half a century and covered the whole of the urban area. This Committee which consisted of 21 nominated members, was classified as a Class-I Committee in the year 1881.

MUNICIPAL CORPORATION OF DELHI

The Delhi Municipal Corporation Act, LXVI of 1957 was enacted by the Parliament on December 28, 1957. Pending the establishment of the Corporation, under a notification of February 15, 1958, issued by the Ministry of Home Affairs, the Government of India appointed, as an interim measure, a Commissioner of Local Authorities to take over the management of all the local bodies to be merged in it. The first general municipal election was held in March, 1958 as a result of the amalgamation of nine of the eleven local bodies and the Delhi District Board, which looked after the civic needs of the rural areas at that time. Only the Delhi Cantonment Board and the New Delhi Municipal Committee continued to exist as independent entities. At the time of establishment of the Corporation in 1958, there were 80 councillors; 12

seats were reserved for the members of the Scheduled Castes. To start with, all the three statutory bodies, which provided water, electricity and transport were converted into Municipal Undertakings and placed under the overall control of the Corporation. After coming under MCD, these were called the Delhi Water Supply & Sewage Disposal Undertaking (DWS & SDU), Delhi Electric Supply Undertaking (DESU) and Delhi Transport Undertaking (DTU), respectively. Later, in the year 1972, a separate Corporation of the central government was formed for facilitating transport activities. Still later, following the implementation of the Delhi Municipal Corporation (Amendment) Act, 1993, separate boards of the Delhi Government were set up in the years 1996 and 1997, respectively and named Delhi Vidyut Board and Delhi Jal Board, respectively.

The year 1963 witnessed decentralisation of the Corporation. A number of the powers, which hitherto rested with the Municipal Corporation and the Commissioner, respectively were delegated to Zonal Committees and Zonal Officers, respectively. The number of councillors was raised from 80 to 100 in 1967. However, the number of Aldermen i.e., six, remained unchanged.

With a view to decentralising municipal services, the Delhi Municipal Corporation Act, 1957 was comprehensively amended in 1993 through a Parliamentary Legislation, namely, The Delhi Municipal Corporation (Amendment) Act, 1993 (Act No. 67 of 1993). It brought about fundamental changes in composition, functions, governance and administration of the Corporation. A basic change that came about was in the composition of the Corporation. The Corporation is composed of Councillors only. They are chosen by direct election, on the basis of adult suffrage, from various wards. The maximum number of total seats of Councillors has been increased to 134. Following are also represented in the Corporation: (a) ten persons, who are not less than 25 years of age and who have special knowledge or experience in municipal administration, to be nominated by the Administrator the persons nominated under this sub-clause have no right to vote in the meetings of the Corporation; and (b) the members of the Lok Sabha representing constituencies, which comprise, wholly or partly, the area of the Corporation and the members of the Rajya Sabha registered as electors within the area of the Corporation; (c) as nearly as may be possible, one-fifth of the members of the Legislative Assembly of Delhi representing constituencies, which comprise wholly or partly, the area of the Corporation to be nominated by the speaker of the Assembly by rotation every year, provided that while nominating such members by rotation, the Speaker shall ensure that, as far as may be possible, all the members are given an opportunity of being represented in the Corporation at least once during the duration of the Corporation; (d) The Chairpersons of the Committees, if any, constituted if they are not Councillors.

The size of the Corporation thus, grew to 272 seats. The number of seats to be reserved for the members of the Scheduled Castes is, as nearly as may be, bears the same ratio to the total number of seats as the population of Scheduled Castes bears to the total population of Delhi. A new concept of rotation of seats has been added, which states that "the seats reserved for Scheduled Castes may be allotted by rotation to different wards in such manner as the Central Government may direct." The concept of reservation of seats for women has been introduced for the first time, with the number of such seats being not less than the one-third of the total number of seats. Such seats reserved for women are allotted by rotation to different wards. Women belonging to Scheduled Castes have been provided a distinct status. It has been stipulated that the number of seats reserved for women belonging to the Scheduled Castes from among the seats reserved for Scheduled Castes shall not be less than one-third of the total number of seats reserved for the Scheduled Castes. The Corporation's tenure, unless it is dissolved earlier than its tenure, is five years from the date appointed for its first meeting. Earlier, the duration of the Corporation was four years and it could remain in supercession for years together. But the amended Act stipulates that an election to constitute the new Corporation shall be completed: (i) before the expiry of its duration or (ii) before the expiry of a period of six months from the date of its dissolution.

DIVIDATION OF MUNICIPAL CORPORATION

The Union government of India on 23 November 2011 approved the Delhi Municipal Corporation (Amendment) Bill 2011, thus paved the way for dividing MCD into 3 corporations and to increase the reservation of seats for women to 50 per cent from the 33 per cent. MCD is Asia's largest civic body. The Bill proposes that MCD (Municipal Corporation of Delhi) should be divided into three separate corporations—East Delhi Municipal Corporation, North Delhi Municipal Corporation, South Delhi Municipal Corporation and 50 per cent reservation for women and three different Mayors for three corporations and setting-up of Directorate of Local Bodies (DLB) which would be headed by director. As per Amendment Bill the civic body in East Delhi will have 64 wards, while the new civic bodies in North and South Delhi will have 104 wards each. Both North and South Delhi municipality will have 26 Assembly constituencies each, while the 16 Assembly segments will be covered under the East Delhi Municipality. The municipal wards would remain 272. As per Amendment Bill, the MHA (Ministry of Home Affairs) would retain supervisory powers that include administrative issues, dissolution of MCD, appointments of Commissioners and Deputy Commissioners and amendments in the Act. Now there are three municipal corporations, one Municipal Council and one Cantonment Board within the National Capital Territory.

STATUTORY COMMITTEES

1. The Standing Committee
2. The Ward Committee
3. The Rural Areas Committee
4. The Education Committee

SPECIAL COMMITTEES AND AD HOC COMMITTEES

As many as the Corporation deems fit.

SUB COMMITTEES

The Standing or the Wards Committee may appoint any Sub-committee from among its own members.

MUNICIPAL COMMISSIONER

The Commissioner is the head of the Executive Wing, assisted by Additional Commissioners (of revenue, education, health, engineering, headquarters, slum and JJ), a Vigilance Director and a Financial Advisor. He is appointed by the central government, which can also remove him on the basis of a resolution passed by three-fifth of the total number of members of the Corporation in a special meeting. The MCD has been divided into 12 zones for administrative convenience. These zones are as follows:

(1) Rohini Zone	(2) West Zone
(3) South Zone	(4) Central Zone
(5) Civil Lines Zone	(6) Karol Bagh Zone
(7) City Zone	(8) Narela Zone
(9) Najafgarh Zone	(10) Shahdara (South) Zone
(11) Shahdara (North) Zone	(12) Sadar Paharganj

The Corporation has been given a wide range of duties and vested with adequate powers. However, the Delhi government and the central government have been given powers of intervention and superintendence. The central Government exercises a good measure of control over the Municipal Corporation, viz, approval of bylaws and regulations, calling for records, reports and accounts, inspection of works, property etc. The Delhi Government has been bestowed with the power to ask for any record, plan or any other document and may depute any person to inspect or examine any Municipal Department or Office of the Corporation. If, in the opinion of the central government, the Corporation is persistently lacking in the performance of the duties given to it, or exceeding or abusing its powers, it may dissolve the Corporation.

The territorial jurisdiction of the MCD, except the small excluded areas of the New Delhi Municipal Council and the Delhi Cantonment Board, is same as that of the Delhi Government, though their respective spheres of activity are different. While the MCD is in-charge of the purely municipal functions, the Delhi Government is responsible for governance of the territory. The Municipal Corporation of Delhi is among the largest municipal bodies in the world, providing civic services to more than estimated population of 1.67 crore citizens in the capital city. It is next only to Tokyo in terms of area. Within its jurisdiction are some of the most densely populated areas in the world. The MCD has been entrusted with 23 obligatory and 27 discretionary functions through which, it touches the lives of citizens round-the-clock, right from birth till death.

OBLIGATORY FUNCTIONS

The functions are as follows: 1.Construction, maintenance and cleaning of drains, drainage works and public latrines, urinals and similar other conveniences. 2.Scavenging, removal and disposal of filth, rubbish and other obnoxious or polluted substances. 3.Reclamation of unhealthy localities, removal of noxious vegetation and abatement of all the nuisances. 4.Regulation of places for the disposal of the dead and the provision and maintenance of places for the said purpose. 5.Registration of births and deaths. 6.Public vaccination and innoculation. 7.Measures for preventing and checking the spread of dangerous diseases. 8.Establishment and maintenance of dispensaries and maternity and child welfare centres and execution of other such activities as may be necessary for public medical relief. 9.Maintenance, including the expansion and upgradation of facilities, of the hospitals existing on the date of the commencement of the DMC (Amendment) Act, 1993. 10.Construction and maintenance of municipal markets and slaughter houses and regulation of all the markets and slaughter houses. 11. The regulation and abatement of offensive or dangerous trades or practices. 12.Possession or removal of dangerous buildings and places. 13.The construction, maintenance, alteration and improvements of public streets, bridges, culverts, causeways etc. 14.Lighting, watering and cleaning of public streets and other public places. 15.Removal of obstructions and projections in or over streets, bridges and other public places. 16.Naming and numbering of streets and premises. 17.Establishment, maintenance of and aid to schools for primary education subject to the condition that such grants may be determined by the central government from time to time. 18.The maintenance of municipal offices. 19.Laying out or maintenance of public parks, gardens and recreation grounds. 20.Maintenance of monuments vested in any local authority in Delhi immediately before the commencement of this Act or, which may be vested in the Corporation after such commencement. 21.The maintenance and development of the value of the properties vested in or entrusted to the management of the Corporation. 22.The preparation of plans for economic development and social justice. 23.The fulfilment of any other obligation imposed by the Act or any other law.

DISCRETIONARY FUNCTIONS

1.Furtherance of education, including cultural and physical education, by measures other than the establishment and maintenance of and aid to schools for primary education. 2.Establishment and maintenance of and aid to libraries, museums, art galleries, botanical and zoological collections. 3.Establishment and maintenance of and aid to stadia, gymnasia, *akharas* and places for sports and games. 4.Planting and care of trees on roadsides and elsewhere 5.Surveys of buildings and land. 6.Registration of marriages. 7.Taking of census of the population. 8.Civic reception to persons of distinction. 9.Providing music or other entertainment modes at public places or places; establishment of theatres and cinemas is also a part of discretionary functions. 10.Organisation and management of fairs and exhibitions. 11.Acquisition of movable or immovable property for any of the purposes mentioned earlier, including the payment of the cost of investigations and surveys of examinations in relation thereto for the construction or adaptation of building necessary for such purposes. 12.The construction and maintenance of: (a) private rest house; (b) houses for the poor; (c) infirmaries; (d) children's homes; (e) houses for the deaf and dumb and also for disabled and handicapped children; (f) shelters for destitute and disabled persons; (g) asylums for persons of unsound mind. 13.Construction and maintenance of cattle compounds. 14.Building, purchase and maintenance of dwelling houses for municipal officers and other municipal employees. 15.Any other measure for the welfare of municipal officers and other municipal employees or any class of them including the sanctioning of loans to such officers and employees or any one of their class for construction of houses and purchase of vehicles. 16.Organisation or management of chemical or bacteriological laboratories for the examination or analysis of water, food and drugs for the detection of diseases or execution of research connected with public health or medical relief. 17.Provision for relief to destitute and disabled persons. 18.Establishment and maintenance of veterinary hospitals. 19.Organisation, construction, maintenance and management of swimming pools, public wash houses, bathing places and other such areas as are designed for the improvement of public health. 20.The organisation and management of farms and dairies within or without Delhi for the supply, distribution and processing of milk and milk products for the benefit of the residents of Delhi. 21.Organisation and management of cottage industries, handicraft centers and sales emporia. 22.Construction and maintenance of warehouses and godowns. 23.Construction and maintenance of garages, sheds and stands of vehicles and cattle biers. 24.Provision of unfiltered water. 25.Improvement of Delhi in accordance with improvement schemes approved by the corporations. 26.Provision of housing accommodation for the inhabitants of any area or for class of inhabitants. 27.Any measure not specifically mentioned, likely to promote public safety, health, convenience or general welfare.

The MCD has the dual responsibility of providing civic services to rural as well as urban areas. It has the responsibility of taking care of rural and urban villages, resettlement colonies, regularised unauthorised colonies, J.J. squatter settlements, slum *basties*, private *katras* etc.

The Corporation levies the following taxes: (a) property taxes; (b) tax on vehicles and animals; (c) theatre tax; (d) tax on advertisements other than advertisements published in the newspapers; (e) duty on the transfer of property; and (f) tax on buildings payable along with the application for sanction of the building plan. In addition to the taxes specified above, the Corporation may levy any of the following taxes: (a) education cess; (b) local tax on land revenues; (c) tax on professionals, trade callings and employment; (d) tax on the consumption (sale or supply) of electricity; (e) betterment tax on the increase in the urban land values caused by the execution of any development or improvement work; (f) a tax on boats; and (g) toll tax.

RURAL AREAS

Rural areas of Delhi have been placed under the territorial jurisdiction of the Municipal Corporation of Delhi. These have also been divided into five Development Blocks, with the Deputy Commissioner functioning as Deputy Development Commissioner under the Development Commissioner. Both of them are responsible for the implementation of development schemes. Moreover, under the Delhi Panchayat Raj Act, 1954, there are Gram Sabhas and Block Panchayats. The provision of civic amenities in rural areas is under the purview of the Municipal Corporation.

NEW DELHI MUNICIPAL COUNCIL

The Raisina Municipal Committee was established in 1916 to cater to the municipal needs of the labour engaged in the construction of India's new capital. It was upgraded to the level of a Second Class municipality to be governed under the Punjab Municipal Act, 1911. Around this time, it was known as Imperial Delhi Municipal Committee. It was named New Delhi Municipal Committee and in 1932, it became a First Class municipality.

In May 1994, the NDMC Act, 1994, replaced the Punjab Municipal Act, 1911 and the Committee was renamed as New Delhi Municipal Council. The Act has been passed by Parliament. For New Delhi Municipal Council, the area under Jurisdiction is about 43 sq. kms. The foreign embassies, Secretariat of the central government and government quarters for the staff are located here. It was felt that "the standards of health, cleanliness, sanitation and education and almost everything" called for special attention and this would not be forthcoming if it were tagged on to a larger body like the MCD. The NDMC area is bounded by the junction of Pusa Road and Upper Ridge Road in the east along New Link Road. It is bounded by Panchkuian Road up to its junction with Old Gurgaon Road. It is bounded in the north-east along Old Gurgaon Road and Chelmsford Road up to the New Delhi Railway Station. It is bounded in the south and south-east along the railway line up to its junction with Hardings Bridge. It is bounded in the south along Mathura Road up to its junction with Lodi Road. It is bounded in the south along the Lodi Road up to its junction with the first road leading to Lodi Colony. It is bounded in the south along the first road leading to Lodi Colony up to its junction with the Ring Railway. It is bounded in the south along the railway line up to its junction with Qutab Road. It is bounded in the south along the Qutab Road up to its junction with Kushak Nalla. It is bounded in the east along the Kushak Nalla up to its junction with the boundary of the Corporation and along the south boundary of the Medical Enclave up to its junction with Ring Road near Gawalior Potteries. It is bounded in the north-west by the Ring Road up to its junction with Kitchner Road. It is bounded in the north along the Upper Ridge.

Council's Members (a) Chairperson, of or above the rank of Joint Secretary to the Government of India appointed by the central government in consultation with the Chief Minister of Delhi; (b) Three members of Legislative Assembly of Delhi representing constituencies, which comprise, wholly or partly, the New Delhi area; (c) Five members from amongst the officers of the central government; and Two members to be nominated by the Central Government in consultation with the Chief Minister of Delhi to represent from among lawyers, doctors, chartered accountants, engineers, business and financial consultants, intellectuals, traders, labourers, social workers, including social scientists, artists, media persons, sportspersons and any other class of persons as may be specified by the central government. The Member of Parliament, representing constituency, which comprises wholly, or partly, the New Delhi Area, is a special invitee for the meetings of the Council but without a right to vote. Out of the eleven members, at least three members are women and one member belongs to the Scheduled Caste. The central government nominates, in consultation with the Chief Minister of Delhi, a Vice-Chairperson from among the members. The Council, unless sooner dissolved, continues for five years from the date appointed for its first meeting and no longer. The Council may constitute as many committees as it deems fit for the exercise of any power or discharge of any function, which the Council may, by a resolution, delegate to them or for inquiring into, reporting or advising upon any matter, which the Council may refer to them. The Chairman is the head of the organisation, the Secretary is the head of the administration and the Financial Advisor looks after the financial control of the civic body. Further, the Chief Auditor has to audit the accounts of expenditure and revenue. There are a number of departments; each department is headed by a senior-level officer, called Head of the Department.

The NDMC has provided high-grade facilities in many spheres of urban life by establishing many prestigious institutions to render essential and standard services to Delhi's citizens. A city is remembered by what one feels while moving through it. The large core of Delhi comprises an area known as Lutyen's Bungalow Zone. It is low-density zone and has been preserved so far for the benefit of 15 lakh people who come for work or otherwise move through everyday. Its wide roads are heavily lined with fully grown trees and almost each inter-section of this area has been developed as a mini garden with a variety of fountains. In addition to providing basic civic amenities to its residents, the Municipal Council also ensures various social, cultural, educational and medical facilities, especially to the government/ municipal employees and other weaker sections of the society. The Act enjoins upon NDMC to take up a role of a mini-government, with all facets of city management except that of policing and transport. It is perhaps the only municipality in the country that supplies electricity and water and its discretionary functions encompass promotion of sports, art, music and culture, maintenance of libraries and care for the old, mentally and physically challenged. The Council has decided to bring art and culture out of the confines of auditoria and museums to open places where general public could also participate in various events related to art and/or culture. It has started organising classical music concert of Morning Raga once in a month at Nehru Park, classical dances at Sur Taal an open air theatre at Talkatora Garden, an open art gallery Srijan at Nehru Park (where budding and eminent artists can create their art forms) and finally, summer vacation workshops for students.

It takes care of working women, housing problems and social facilities like *barat ghars* and community centres.

DELHI CANTONMENT BOARD

The setting up the Delhi Cantonment Board was justified on the grounds of security and public interest. The Delhi Cantonment Board has also been excluded from the jurisdiction of the Municipal Corporation of Delhi. It extends over an area of 43 sq. kms., located in south and south-west of Delhi. It has seven officials and seven elected members. The Board attends to normal municipal activities, except those coming under the direct responsibility of the military authorities. Most of the population belongs to armed forces and the civilian population and the number of their houses is less.

■ OTHER IMPORTANT ORGANISATIONS ■

DELHI DEVELOPMENT AUTHORITY

While the town development should have been the responsibility of the Delhi Municipal Corporation, the Government of India felt that a Master

Plan for the development of the city on sound lines had to be drawn up. Besides, the development of vast areas to give relief to the overcrowded city would present problems of the highest complexity. Hence, due attention to the subject could be given only by having a special body constituted for this purpose only. Consequently, the Delhi Development Authority was constituted with an objective, "to provide for the development of Delhi according to plan and for matters ancillary thereto." The Lieutenant-Governor of Delhi is its ex-officio Chairman while its members, besides others (appointed by the Central Government) are—the Commissioner of Municipal Corporation of Delhi (ex-officio), three representatives of the State Assembly and nominees of the Central Government. The association of the representatives of the Municipal Corporation (including the Municipal Commissioner) and that of the MLAs is intended to provide for coordinating the programmes of the DDA with the requirements of development of Delhi. Its Vice-Chairman, Finance Member and Engineer Member are appointed by the central government. The Advisory Council attached to the Authority comprises 20 members, including the Chairman of the DDA who is its ex-officio President. Ten of its members are nominated by the central government out of which, four are from its technical departments, three are the Members of Parliament and others are representatives from Delhi Transport Corporation, Municipal Corporation of Delhi and its Electric and Water Supply and Sewage Disposal Committees and Commerce, Industry and Labour representatives. The main functions of the DDA are: (a) acquisition and development of land; and (b) activities connected with improvement of housing and slums.

TOWN AND COUNTRY PLANNING ORGANISATION

This organisation drew up a Master Plan for Delhi in 1957 in consultation with the DDA and got it approved by the central government. Delhi was the first city in India to have a comprehensive Master Plan, which takes into account the metropolitan and regional development proposals. The detailed implementation of the Plan is the concern of a number of bodies, namely the Delhi Government, the Municipal Corporation of Delhi and its statutory undertakings, the New Delhi Municipal Council, the Public Works Department of the Central Government and the Central Ministry of Works, Housing and Urban Development. However, primarily, an overall responsibility for its success lies with the Delhi Development Authority.

DELHI URBAN ARTS COMMISSION

The Delhi Urban Arts Commission, which has been set up under an Act of Parliament of 1973, is vested with the responsibility of maintenance of urban design and aesthetic standards and environment in Delhi. Other agencies such as the DDA, MCD, NDMC and Cantonment Board are also expected to conform to standards of urban design while undertaking construction activities on their own or sanctioning or approving plans for buildings, offices, parks, entertainment centres etc. However, it has been felt that the Delhi Urban Arts Commission has not been effective in its functioning, as it has no powers to enforce its decisions or penalise defaulters. As the actual sanctions are issued by other bodies and agencies, its control is deemed inadequate.

NATIONAL CAPITAL REGION PLANNING BOARD

Delhi's growth is not confined to the boundaries of the Union Territory alone. Its urban spatial expansion has spread into the surrounding areas of U.P. and Haryana like Faridabad, Ballabhgarh and Gurgaon in Haryana and Ghaziabad and Noida in Uttar Pradesh. For achieving the objective of planned development of Delhi, a regional approach was adopted to plan the National Capital Region (NCR) in as early as 1957 during the preparation of the Master Plan for Delhi by the erstwhile Town Planning Organisation. A planning board for the development of the National Capital Region has been set up with the consent of the participating states of the region, viz., Haryana, Rajasthan and U.P. and the Union Territory of Delhi in 1985. The Union Minister of Urban Development is the ex-officio Chairman of the board, which has twenty-one members, besides five co-opted members and representatives of various concerned ministries of the Government of India, Chief Ministers and Ministers in-charge of Urban Development in the constituent states and the Lieutenant Governor and finally, the Chief Minister of Delhi.

The National Capital Region was established in recognition of the growing interdependencies of the larger metropolitan area around the city. This region is the most urbanized region and faces problem of unplanned and haphazard development in Delhi and the adjoining areas. The National Capital Region Planning Board prepared a statutory regional plan (2001) for the region. Its goals was to balance the harmonious development, leading to dispersal of economic activities and the population. Planners and policy makers had sensed the need for a unified legal framework to achieve a unified capital region. The vital goals of National Capital Region are: (a) well organized urban places in National Capital Region in a physically efficient pattern and socially desirable environment with effective participation of the local units that will sustain dynamic growth in tune with the national goals; (b) rational and orderly growth of Delhi as the beautiful national capital, symbolizing life and aspiration of the nation; (c) an integrated and coordinated development of the transport system, drainage and power supply of the region, within a broad regional network; (d) healthy rural and urban relationship with protection of the freshness of air and water in the region; (e) sustained development planning of the region and the effective implementation of the plan in close integration with eco-development of the country with a suitable organizational machinery.

3 MORE DISTRICTS ENTER NCR FOLD

The National Capital Region has undergone another expansion with

three more districts—Mahendragarh and Bhiwani (both in Haryana) and Bharatpur (Rajasthan)—added to it on July 1, 2013. This brings the number of districts in the NCR to 19, with the total area increasing by 34% to 46,249 sq km. The expansion would help in dispersal of economic activities and reduce pressure on Delhi's health educational and economic infrastructure.

Refer map that follows. It shows that constituent areas of the NCR.

MASTER PLAN FOR DELHI-2001

The perspective Plan-2001 ensures an appropriate balance between the spatial allocations for the distribution of housing, employment, social infrastructure, shopping centers, public and individual transport networks and adequate arrangements to accommodate different types of physical infrastructure and public utility systems. The concept underlying the perspective Plan is as follows:

(1) Delhi to be planned as an integral part of its region.

(2) Ecological balance to be maintained.

(3) The central city area to be treated as Special Area.

(4) Urban Heritage of Delhi to be conserved.

(5) The city center to be decentralized.

(6) The mass transport system to be multi-model.

(7) Urban development to be of a low rise high density type.

(8) Urban development to be hierarchical.

▌ DISTRICT ADMINISTRATION ▌

After independence, the nature of district administration underwent some changes with devolution of powers to the newly created departments. For example, the Municipality evolved into the MCD, in which the DC had no role to play after 1958. The development works were transferred to the Development Commissioner, the industries work to the Directorate of Industries and the work of transport to the Department of Transport.

However, the D.C. of Delhi continued to be the Head of the District Administration. He was responsible for law and order, excise, issue of licenses for arms and explosives and citizenship certificates, apart from revenue and criminal judicial work. During the mid-seventies, the DC's office was organized as follows. There were four administrative districts - New, Central, North and South, looked after by three ADMs. Among these various other powers and functions. The such as treasuries, excise, entertainment etc. were divided. ADM's, Revenue and Land Acquisition tasks were supervised by the ADM (Revenue) and the ADM (LA), respectively. There were 12 sub-divisions, each headed by one SDM, which was later reduced to seven.

Two major changes greatly diluted the role of the DC Office. The first one was the separation of the executive and the judiciary in 1969 after which heinous crimes were dealt with by; Sessions Courts but other offences, including IPC offences, were dealt with by Judicial Magistrates. The Executive Magistrates were required to look after executive and administrative matters such as licensing, sanction of prosecution and preventive sections of the C.P.C. In 1978, the Delhi Police Act was promulgated by which, Delhi came under the system of the Commissioner of Police. Almost all the powers of the District Magistrates as per the C.P.C. were vested in the Police Commissioner. Section 107 and Section 144 C.P.C., which are very important vis-a-vis law and order have been directly dealt with by the Police since then. Furthermore, powers of licensing and entertainment, that were hitherto vested in the D.C. were also given to the Police.

This was the situation in 1996 when the exercise of decentralizing the DC's office, by setting up 27 SDM offices and 9 DC offices, was started. While the SDMs were put in place during the middle of 1996, the DCs began functioning from January 1, 1997. All the Deputy Commissioners report to the Divisional Commissioner.

ORGANISATIONAL SETUP

Delhi has been divided into 11 Districts:

District	Sub Divisions		
1. Central Delhi	Civil Lines	Kotwali	Karol Bagh
2. North Delhi	Model Town	Narela	Alipur
3. South Delhi	Saket	Mehrauli	Hauz Khas
4. East Delhi	Gandhi Nagar	Preet Vihar	Mayur Vihar
5. North-East Delhi	Seelampur	Yamuna Vihar	Karawal Nagar
6. South-West Delhi	Dwarka	Najafgarh	Kapasheda
7. New Delhi	Delhi Cantonment	Vasant Vihar	Chankyapuri
8. North-West Delhi	Saraswati Vihar	Rohini	Kanjhawala
9. West Delhi	Patel Nagar	Punjabi Bagh	Rajouri Garden
10. South-East Delhi	Defence Colony	Kalkaji	Sarita Vihar
11. Shahdara	Shahdara	Seemapuri	Vivek Vihar

Each District is headed by a Deputy Commissioner. There are 33 Sub-Divisions in entire Delhi. Every district has three Sub-Divisions. Each Sub-Division is headed by a Sub-Divisional Magistrate. All the Deputy Commissioners report to the Divisional Commissioner. The government increased the districts of Delhi to 11, each headed by a Deputy Commissioner, for more efficient and effective district administration. It holds People's Courts and Consumer Courts.

■ POLICE ■

Delhi has a long history of policing through the famed institution of the Kotwal. Malikul Umara Faqruddin is said to be the first Kotwal of Delhi in 1237 A.D. who was also simultaneously appointed as the Naibe-Ghibat (Regent in Absence). It is presumed that the Kotwal, or Police Head quarters was then located at Qila Rai Pithora or today's Mehrauli. When emperor Shahjahan shifted his capital from Agra to Delhi in 1648, he appointed Ghaznafar Khan as the first Kotwal of the new city, also bestowing on him the responsibilities of an important office the Mir-i-Atish (Chief of Artillery).

The institution of Kotwal came to an end with the crushing of the 1857 revolt by the British. And, interestingly, the last Kotwal of Delhi, appointed just before the eruption of the revolt, was Gangadhar Nehru, father of Pandit Motilal Nehru and grand father of Pandit Jawaharlal Nehru. An organised form of policing was established by the British after 1857, with the adoption of the Indian Police Act of 1861. Delhi being a part of the Punjab, remained a unit of the Punjab Police even after becoming the capital of India in 1912. In the same year, the first Chief Commissioner of Delhi was appointed and was vested with the powers and functions of the Inspector General of Police. The Delhi District was then, under the control of a DIG of Police, with his headquarters at Ambala. The police force in the Delhi district was commanded by a Superintendent and a Deputy Superintendent of Police. The total composition of the force then, was — 2 Inspectors, 27 Sub-inspectors, 110 Head Constables, 985 Foot Constables and 28 Sawars. In the city, the rural police was under in the charge of two Inspectors, with their headquarters at Sonepat and Ballabgarh, respectively. They had 10 police stations under their control. In addition, there were 7 outposts and four 'road posts'. In the city, there were three large police stations of Kotwali, Subzi Mandi and Paharganj. In Civil Lines, there were spacious police barracks where the Reserve Armed Reserve policemen and recruits were accommodated.

POST-INDEPENDENCE: POLICE SET-UP

Delhi Police was reorganised in 1946 when its strength was almost doubled. In the wake of partition, a large influx of refugee population entered the city and there was a sharp rise in the number of crimes in 1948. The total strength of the Delhi Police was increased by 1951 to about 8000, with one Inspector General of Police and eight Superintendents of Police. With the rise in the population of Delhi, the strength of the Delhi Police kept on increasing and in the year 1961, it was over 12000. In the year 1966, the Government of India constituted the Delhi Police Commission, which was headed by Justice G.D.Khosla to look into the problems faced by Delhi Police. It was on the basis of the Commission's Report that the Delhi Police was once again reorganised. Four Police Districts, namely, North, Central, South and New Delhi, were constituted. The Commission also recommended the introduction of a Police Commissioner System, which was eventually adopted from July 1,1978. Under the system, the responsibility for all the aspects of policing vests in the Commissioner. In order to fulfil this responsibility, the Commissioner is vested with powers of regulation, control, licensing etc., in addition to the usual police powers enjoyed by him. The police officers exercise certain powers that are normally exercisable by Executive Magistrates. Section 107 and Section 144 of C.P.C., which are very important for maintaining law and order, have since then, been directly dealt with by the Police. Furthermore, the powers of licensing and entertainment, which were earlier vested in the D.C., were also given to the Police.

The organisation of the police force is more or less on the lines of those of other metropolitan cities, viz., Mumbai, Kolkatta and Chennai, with a Commissioner of Police at the helm of affairs and an hierarchical structure. But, unlike other state capitals, the elected representatives of Delhi are not empowered to take decisions on matters relating to public order and police. As a reserved subject, the Lieutenant-Governor acts on his discretion while dealing with these matters but under the control of the central government.

ORGANISATIONAL SET-UP

The population of Delhi and the problems of policing kept on multiplying and following the recommendations of the Srivastava Committee, the strength of the Delhi Police was increased to the present level of 83,762. At present, there are 6 ranges, 14 districts and 184 police stations in Delhi. Today, the Delhi Police is perhaps the largest metropolitan police in the world, larger than those of London, Paris, New York and Tokyo in terms of number.

The Police Commissioner is assisted by Joint Commissioners and Additional Commissioners while exercising his powers and performing of his duties. Each police district is placed under the charge of a Deputy Commissioner of Police (DCP) who is assisted by one or more additional DCPs. The DCPs are empowered to hold externalisation proceedings against the habitual offenders under Sections 47 and 48 of the Act. However, their actions can be challenged in the higher courts of law. Likewise, each police subdivision is placed under the charge of an Assistant Commissioner of Police (ACP) and each police station under the charge of an Inspector of Police. The ACPs are empowered to conduct security proceedings under Section 107 of the C.P.C. The action under this head is of preventive nature only and can be challenged in all the Sessions/High Courts. The ACPs being the Special Executive Magistrates, are also accountable to the Sessions Court rather than to their respective parent departments. Then comes the SHO, the incharge of a police station. He has the rank of an Inspector and is assisted by an additional SHO (who is also an inspector). The police station is manned by Sub-Inspectors, Assistant Sub-Inspectors, Head Constables and Constables.

Joint Commissioners : 20   Additional Commissioners : 20

- **Different Wings of the Delhi Police:** Economic Offences, Crime, these are — Railways, Licensing, Narcotics and Crime Prevention Cell, Crime Against Women Cell, Special Branch, Special Cell, Special Riot Cell, Vigilance etc.

- **Police Ranges and Districts**
  Total Ranges : 06   Total Districts : 14

1. **Districts in the New Delhi Range:** New Delhi District, Metro and Railway.

2. **Districts in the Northern Range:** North-West District, Outer District.

3. **Districts in the South Eastern Range :** South District, South East District

4. **Districts of South Western Range :** West District, South West District.

5. **Districts of Eastern Range :** East District, North-East District.

6. **Districts of Central Range :** Central and North Districts.

POLICE STATIONS IN DELHI

- **South District:** 1. Defence Colony 2. Lodhi Colony 3. Kotla Mubarak Pur 4. Hauz Khas 5. Malviya Nagar 6. Saket 7. Mehrauli 8. Fatehpur Beri 9. Neb Sarai 10. Vasant Vihar 11. Vasant Kunj North 12. Vasant Kunj South 13. South Campus 14. Safdarjung Enclave 15. R.K. Puram 16. Sarojini Nagar.
- **South-East District:** 1. New Friends Colony 2. Jamia Nagar 3. H.N. Din 4. Sunlight Colony 5. Lajpat Nagar 6. Amar Colony 7. Greater Kailash 8. Kalkaji 9. Govind Puri 10. Okhla Ind. Area 11. Sarita Vihar 12. Badarpur 13. Jaitpur 14. Ambedkar Nagar 15. Sangam Vihar 16. Chitranjan Park 17. Pul Prahlad Pur.
- **South-West District:** 1. Delhi Cantt. 2. Inder Puri 3. Naraina 4. Sector 23 Dwarka 5. Dwarka North 6. Kapashera 7. Dwarka South 8. Dabri 9. Palam Village 10. Binda Pur 11. Sagar Pur 12. Najafgarh 13. Jaffarpur Kalan 14. Chhawla 15. Baba Haridas Nagar.
- **West District:** 1. Tilak Nagar 2. Hari Nagar 3. Maya Puri 4. Vikas Puri 5. Janak Puri 6. Uttam Nagar 7. Rajouri Garden 8. Kirti Nagar 9. Khyala 10. Moti Nagar 11. Punjabi Bagh 12. Paschim Vihar 13. Mianwali Nagar 14. Nangloi 15. Nihal Vihar 16. Ranhola 17. Mundka.
- **New Delhi District:** 1. Parliament Street 2. Mandir Marg 3. Connaught Place 4. Barakhamba Road 5. Tilak Marg 6. Chankaya Puri 7. Tuglak Road.
- **East District:** 1. Gandhi Nagar 2. Geeta Colony 3. Krishna Nagar 4. Vivek Vihar 5. Anand Vihar 6. Farash Bazar 7. Preet Vihar 8. Jagat Puri 9. Shakar Pur 10. Madhu Vihar 11. Mandawali 12. Pandav Nagar 13. Kalyan Puri 14. New Ashok Nagar 15. Mayur Vihar 16. Ghazipur.
- **North-East District:** 1. Seelampur 2. Zafrabad 3. New Usman Pur 4. Khajuri Khas 5. Sonia Vihar 6. Karawal Nagar 7. Gokul Puri 8. Bhajanpura 9. Jyoti Nagar 10. Shahadra 11. Mansarover Park 12. Welcome 13. Seema Puri 14. Nandnagri 15. G.T.B. Enclave 16. Harsh Vihar.
- **North District:** 1. Civil Lines 2. Maurice Nagar 3. Timar Pur 4. Burari 5. Sarai Rohilla 6. Gulabi Bagh 7. Roop Nagar 8. Sadar Bazar 9. Bara Hindu Rao 10. Subzi Mandi 11. Kotwali 12. Lahori Gate 13. Kashmere Gate.
- **Central District**: 1. Darya Ganj 2. Chandni Mahal 3. Jama Masjid 4. Kamla Market 5. Hauz Qazi 6. I.P. Estate 7. Pahar Ganj 8. Nabi Karim 9. D.B.G. Road 10. Karol Bagh 11. Parshad Nagar 12. Rajinder Nagar 13. Patel Nagar 14. Ranjit Nagar 15. Anand Parbat.
- **North-West District**: 1. Ashok Vihar 2. Bharat Nagar 3. Keshav Puram 4. Subhash Place 5. Maurya Enclave 6. Rani Bagh 7. Model Town 8. Adarsh Nagar 9. Mukherji Nagar 10. Shalimar Bagh 11. Mahendra Park 12. Jahangir Puri 13. Swarup Nagar 14. Bhalswa Dairy.
- **Outer District**: 1. Alipur 2. Narela 3. Vijay Vihar 4. South Rohini 5. Mangol Puri 6. Sultan Puri 7. Aman Vihar 8. Begum Pur 9. Bawana 10. Kanjhawala 11. Shahbad Dairy 12. Samaipur Badli 13. K.N. Katju Marg 14. Prashant Vihar 15. North Rohini.
- **Crime & RLYS**: 1. Delhi Main Railway Station 2. New Delhi Railway Station 3. Sarai Rohilla 4. Hazrat Nizamuddin 5. Anand Vihar Rly. Station.
- **Metro Police Stations**: 1. Shastri Park Metro 2. Rithala Metro 3. Kashmere Gate Metro 4. Raja Garden Metro 5. Yamuna Depot Metro 6. Qutab Minar Metro 7. Kalkaji Mandir Metro 8. IGI Airport Metro
- **Airport Police Stations**: 1. Domestic Airport 2. IGI Airport

Note: Apart from above, following 5 Units declared as Police Stations are also functioning in Delhi for specialized crimes having jurisdiction all over Delhi: 1. PS Special Cell, 2. PS Economic Offences Wing (EOW), 3. PS CAW Cell, 4. PS Crime Branch, 5. PS Vigilance Unit

DELHI TOURIST POLICE

Delhi is an important tourist destination and also a transit point wherefrom international and national tourist make future journey to various other tourist places. Tourist at times face several problems related to transport, accommodation, getting tourism related information and many times they fall victim to cheats and touts losing their belongings and valuables. To help tourists, the tourist Police of the Delhi Police shall be deployed at following ten important places/locations:

1. IGI Airport
2. New Delhi Railway Station
3. Hazrat Nizammuddin Railway Station
4. Raj Ghat
5. Red Fort
6. Qutub Minar
7. Palika Bazar
8. Janpath
9. India Gate
10. Pahar Ganj (Railway Station Side)

OBJECTIVE: *1.* To avoid harassment to the tourist by touts. *2.* To help tourist in getting transport and lodging at appropriate rate and without much hassle at Railway Station, Airports Bus Terminals, important tourist places, malls etc. *3.* Safety and security against cheats and bag lifters etc. at these places. *4.* Containing crime like pick pocketing, eve-teasing, molestation, drugging etc. *5.* Providing information related to the Capital of Delhi and other adjoining tourist places.

DUTIES: *1.* To guide the tourist about the location of tourist places, distance and available transport to reach desired destination. *2.* To help tourist in procuring tickets for museums, resorts, transports, movies and also to protect them from touts and black marketers. *3.* To ensure that no peddlers, jewelers, shopkeepers, touts, cheats and beggars etc. harass them. *4.* To help tourists in solving their problems as also facilitating them during stay in the city. *5.* To guide tourists about local of Art and Culture, Emporia's, Book Stalls, Banks, PCOs etc. *6.* To guide tourists on local conditions of law and order, security and hazards and places of medical help. *7.* To guide the tourists on matters relating to passport, visas, residential permits exchange of currency and on immigration issues. *8.* To help sorting out matters of exigency like sickness, loss of theft of belonging assault or involvement in criminal cases. *9.* To guide local custom and tradition.

❒ ❒ ❒

5 Public Finance

CONSTITUTIONALLY, Delhi is a Union Territory with Legislature. However special provisions made in the Constitution (Article 259 AA) and the National Capital Territory Act 1991 have given Delhi a special status distinct from the States and other Union Territories. The Legislative Assembly of Delhi has been given the same powers in financial matters, as have been enshrined in the Constitution for State except Public Order, Police and Land which rest with the Government of India. Unlike the States, the Annual Financial Statement or the Budget of Delhi requires prior approval of not only the Lt. Governor but also the President of India before it can be presented to the State Legislature for consideration and passing.

Delhi Government's Revenue Receipts Consist of Tax Revenue, Non-Tax Revenue, Grants-in-Aid and Compensation (due to the implementation of GST) from the centre.

PLAN OUTLAY

The Plan outlay and expenditure under various Five Year Plans are indicated below:

Sl. N.	Five Year Plan	Approved Outlay	Total Plan Exp.
1.	I Five Year Plan 1951-1956	6.30	4.70
2.	II Five Year Plan 1956-1961	17.00	15.37
3.	III Five Year Plan 1961-1966	99.33	93.10
4.	IV Five Year Plan 1969-1974	168.77	155.16
5.	V Five Year Plan 1974-1979	363.75	341.34
6.	VI Five Year Plan 1980-1985	1039.38	1041.95
7.	VII Five Year Plan 1985-1990	2537.34	2631.47
8.	VIII Five Year Plan 1992-1997	4500.00	6208.32
9.	IX Five Year Plan 1997-2002	15541.28	13465.09
10.	X Five Year Plan 2002-2007	23000.00	22646.00
11.	XI Five Year Plan 2007-2012	54799.00	53478.86
12.	XII Five Year Plan 2012-2017	90000.00	40574.53

* (Exp. for 2007-08 & 2008-09).

PUBLIC FINANCE : SOME FACTS

- As per the provision of Government of NCT of Delhi Act, 1991, a Consolidated Fund, separate from that of the Government of India, had been constituted with effect from December 1993. All revenue and capital receipts of the Delhi Government are being credited in this fund and all govt. expenditure under Scheme/ Programme/ Projects and Establishment are being met from this fund.

- Delhi Government's Revenue Receipts consist of Tax Revenue, Non-Tax Revenue, Grants-in-Aid and compensation (due to the implementation of GST) from the Centre. The Tax Revenue includes receipts under SGST/Value Added Tax (VAT), Stamps and Registration Fees, State Excise and Motor Vehicle Tax. On the other hand, its Non Tax Revenue mainly comprises Interest Receipts, Dividend and Profit from investments and Service Charges/Fees/Fines, etc. from various government departments and various public sector undertakings.

- The Grants-in-Aid from the Centre includes: (i) Grant in lieu of Share in Central Taxes, enhanced compensation to 1984 riot victims, compensation to Jammu and Kashmir Migrants and (ii) Normal Central Assistance and grant in aid for Centrally Sponsored Schemes, Central Road Fund.

- Similarly, the Delhi Government's Capital Receipts mainly cover the recovery of loans and advances from Local Bodies/Undertakings/ Government Servants, etc. and Small Savings Loans from National Small Savings Fund (NSSF) of the Government of India.

- The expenditure from the Consolidated Fund of Delhi is broadly maintained under the Heads of Establishment and Scheme/ Programme/ Projects including Centrally Sponsored Scheme (CSS).Further, both the Establishment and Scheme/ Programme/ Projects expenditure is maintained under the Heads of Revenue and Capital Account. The classification of expenditure into Plan and Non Plan was removed in the financial year of 2017-18 and now there is only Revenue and Capital Classification.

❏ ❏ ❏

6 Education Infrastructure

EDUCATION holds the key to economic growth, social transformation, modernization and national integration. Delhi has been a great centre of learning and education for centuries. However, the tradition of learning and education was firmly established in Delhi when the Sultanate made the city its headquarters (1206-1526). During the medieval period, the curriculum set for students, though not uniform, was limited and Islamic education comprised mainly Arabic, Persian, Turkish, Logic, Medicine, Theology, Ethics, History and Grammar. In the ancient Indian studies, the emphasis was on Vedanta (philosophy) and Patanjali. Under the Sultanate, many a madrasas was set up. Amir Khusrau and his spiritual master, Hazrat Nizamuddin Auliya, contributed much to the scholarly life of Delhi. Literary societies were formed. The Khiljis and Tughlaks also set up many madrasas, which were attached to mosques.

> At present, Delhi's Literacy Rate (86.2) is higher than the national average. Close to 86% of Delhi's population is literate, higher than the national average of 73%.

EDUCATION BEFORE INDEPENDENCE

With the passage of time, the famous centres of learning floundered due to the political vicissitudes through which, Delhi passed. Many old institutions languished for want of funds; the majority of children, who used to attend schools due to financial support from an affluent person, found no patrons; and teachers were also inadequately paid. Only a few education institutions managed to exist against all odds. During the early nineteenth century, 147 native schools were situated in Delhi and its vicinity. Out of these schools, 40 were Hindu schools and 103 Muslim schools. Further, college education began during the late nineteenth century.

Delhi College

Delhi College was started originally as Madrasa Ghaziuddin in a sarai in 1792. It was taken over by the British administration in 1825 and English, Mathematics and other subjects were added to its curriculum. The course of study could be pursued through English or Urdu language. Following the mutiny, it ceased to exist in 1857. The college building was occupied by troops for many years afterwards. The college was revived in February, 1872 for the purpose of promoting the study of English language among the citizens of Delhi. After 1877, it was reorganised as Anglo-Arabic School. It was raised to degree level and later, affiliated to Delhi University in 1924. Further, M.A. classes were introduced in 1941 and the school was separated from the college. Delhi College suffered during the communal riots of 1947 but was again reorganised in 1948 with its old name of Delhi College. It is now a constituent college of Delhi University, known as Zakir Hussain College.

St. Stephen's School

The first English institution in Delhi, St. Stephen's Mission High School was opened shortly after 1857 in collaboration with the S.G.P. Mission, Delhi.

Other Institutions

In 1881, a Tibbia school was established by Hakim Abdul Majid Khan to give instructions in the main Unani system of medicine. St. Stephen's College founded in 1865, was affiliated to the Punjab University in 1882; Hindu college was founded in 1899 for the purpose of giving education according to the principles of Sanatan Sabha. In 1916, Lady Hardinge College started its course in medical science. Finally, Ramjas College was founded in 1917.

GROWTH OF MODERN EDUCATION

The Delhi Municipality introduced compulsory primary education in two wards of the city from April, 1925, which was subsequently extended to other areas. Generous funds were provided in the form of grants to privately managed schools. A high school examination system was initiated, which supplanted the Punjab Matriculation Examination. Governments educational grants to the District Boards, Imperial Delhi Municipal Committee and Notified Area Committee of Delhi also promoted the cause of education.

The National Policy on Education, formulated in 1986 and modified in 1992, aims to provide education of a comparable quality up to a given level to all students irrespective of the criterion of caste, creed, residence or gender. It aims at promoting nationalism, inculcating the thoughts of common citizenship and composite culture and strengthening national integration. The thrust in elementary education is on: (i) universal enrolment and universal retention of children upto 14 years of age; and (ii) a substantial improvement in the quality of education.

In Delhi, educational facilities are provided in stages, i.e., pre-primary, primary, middle, secondary, senior secondary and university levels. Pre-primary and primary education is the responsibility of the local bodies. Middle, secondary and senior secondary education is primarily looked after by the Delhi Government. Although pre-primary and primary education is mainly the responsibility of the local bodies, yet the Delhi Government has converted its 343 schools into composite schools, now known as Sarvodaya Vidyalayas, having classes from I to XII. At the university level, the Delhi Government is running several degree colleges, funded by UGC and Delhi Govt. NDMC, though mainly concerned with primary education, is also running a selected number of middle, secondary and senior secondary schools in its areas. Apart from this a number of private organizations are also engaged in imparting education at all levels of schooling. These organizations are given grant-in-aid by the Delhi Government to meet the expenditure on education. Besides these, recognised unaided schools are also being run in Delhi by registered trusts and societies.

PRIMARY EDUCATION

After independence, the first Plan laid great emphasis on primary education. The passing of the Delhi Primary Education Act by the Indian Parliament in 1950 led to an unprecedented expansion of educational facilities. The number of primary schools went up from 1726 in 1980-81 to 2745 in 2017-18. Primary classes are also being run in 385 Sarvodaya Vidyalays of the Delhi Government. Physical education now forms a part of primary and secondary education. The responsibility of primary education was shared by the Delhi Government, Municipal Committee, NDMC, Notified Area Committees and the Cantonment Board.

With the setting up of Delhi Municipal Corporation in 1958, all the primary schools except New Delhi and the cantonment Area, were placed under it. In 1960, primary education was made free and compulsory for all children. Committed to improve the standard of nursery and primary education for the harmonious development of children, the M.C.D. provides facilities like free school uniforms, textbooks, mid-day meals, health cover, scholarships, physical education, science education, excursions and educational trips. It also takes care of teachers' professional growth.

SECONDARY EDUCATION

Prior to 1970, the responsibility of imparting secondary education did not rest with any single agency. In 1970, Delhi Administration took over the responsibility of over 413 middle and 11 higher secondary schools from the Delhi Municipal Corporation under its unified control. In order to avoid duplication of facilities, whenever a higher secondary school was opened, the middle school was discontinued. Now, the overall administration of education lies with the Directorate of Education, Delhi Government. There has been a rapid expansion of secondary education in Delhi. The number of middle schools in Delhi is 905 and secondary/ senior secondary schools 2110. Instruction through correspondence has also been introduced. The government has opened separate schools for boys and girls as well as for co-educational schools. The same infrastructure, including building, is used for running two schools, with the girls coming in the first shift and the boys (in the afternoon) for the second shift. Since 1961, great emphasis has been placed on teaching of sciences. The courses of study at higher secondary stages are specific and oriented towards such disciplines as science, commerce, humanities, home science and agriculture. Students can opt for a technical course in a technical school or a vocational course along with academic courses in a selected school.

Super Ability Schools

The Government of Delhi has launched an innovative scheme of Super Ability Schools, called Pratibha Vikas Vidyalayas. The idea behind this project is to provide the best possible environment, education and guidance to the potential leaders of the country who otherwise get lost in the crowd because of their economic handicaps as they cannot afford to pay the rising costs of education in public schools.

SCERT

On May 27, 1988, the State Council of Educational Research and Training (SCERT) was set up in Delhi to look after in-service training and other activities of teachers with inputs, cooperation and involvement of the National Council of Educational Research and Training (NCERT). This has resulted in great benefit for Delhi's teachers and educational functionaries. Under these programmes, a number of teachers have had an opportunity to travel to other states, participate in the programmes conducted by the NCERT, reap a rich harvest of increasing their academic calibre and knowing other parts of their nation.

DELHI SKILL DEVELOPMENT MISSION

Skill up-gradation is essential to meet the requirement of trained and skilled manpower of the industrial and service sectors. Accordingly it was decided to set up a State Level Skill Development Mission to provide intersectoral co-ordination at the state level by Government of Delhi under the Chairmanship of Hon'ble Chief Minister. Delhi Skill Development Mission was registered on 12th June, 2009 under the Societies Act, 1860. The Mission is to provide skill development training to the students passing out from schools, unemployed youth and drop-outs, informal sector workers. At present various schemes/activities are simultaneously running under the aegis of Delhi Skill Mission in the field of imparting training, granting certification, quality improvement and introduction of new scheme, courses and institutes. Delhi Skill Development Mission, aims to train about one lakh person per year.

VOCATIONAL EDUCATION IN SCHOOLS

The Directorate of Education, Delhi started Vocational Education Programme in 1977-78. At present, 17 Vocational courses based on Engineering and Technology, Business and Commerce, Home-science, Health and Para-medical, Agriculture, Computer and other miscellaneous streams are taught at the +2 stage.

COMPUTER EDUCATION PROGRAMME (ICT)

Under ICT scheme of the Ministry of HRD, GoI, it is proposed to set up new computer labs in all Delhi Govt. schools for computer Education at Sr. Secondary level and computer literacy programme for other students. This Programme is being jointly funded by Govt. of India and Govt. of Delhi in the ratio of 75:25. This programme provides two computers, furniture, broadband connectivity, peripherals and one IT assistant for each school as well as branches. Further, funds are provided for strengthening and maintenance of MIS (Management Information System) application.

RIGHT TO EDUCATION ACT

The Right of Children to Free and Compulsory Education (RTE) Act, 2009 provides children in the 6-14 age group the legal entitlement to free and compulsory education. It lays down norms and standards for infrastructure, PTRs for the primary and upper primary stage of education and academic responsibilities of teachers. It is obligatory under the Act for Private School to admit 25% of Students from poor families and Govt shall re-imburse expenditure so incurred by it to the extent of per-child expenditure incurred by the State on education, or the actual amount charged from the child, whichever is less. Govt. of Delhi started reimbursing @ ₹ 1190/- per student per month since 2011-12 to the private schools for students admitted under EWS quota or RTE Act, 2009.

MENSTRUAL HYGIENE AMONG ADOLESCENT GIRLS IN SCHOOL (KISHORI)

Under the scheme, one pack of sanitary napkin is provided every month to all girl students from classes VI to XII in Govt. and Aided School. Around 7.00 lakh girls students of Govt. and Govt. aides schools are benefitted under this plan scheme.

VIDYALAYA KALYAN SAMITI (V.K.S.)

To encourage people's participation in Management of Govt. Schools, VKS has been constituted for each school. Besides, the head of schools, members have been nominated from PTA, RWA and NGO working in that area. In order to strengthen VKS, budgetary allocation has been enhanced to ₹ 4.00 lakh per year for each school.

MID-DAY MEAL

Mid-day Meal Programme is one of the successful programmes in Delhi. In November 2001, Supreme Court directed to the States to provide 'cooked food' to every child in government and government-aided primary schools with a minimum of 300 calories and 8-12 grams of protein each day of school for a minimum of 200 days in a year. Till 2004-05, cooked meal was served in schools run by Government and Local Bodies. The programme has been extended to Government aided schools from 2005-06. Provision of ₹ 2 per day per child spend on Mid-day Meal for students of Primary classes, was raised to ₹ 2.50 per day per child from 2008-09. The scheme has been extended to students of upper primary classes (upto VIII). Under revised guidelines issued by the Government of India, minimum calories are raised from 300 to 450 per day.

YUVA

Objectives:

- To make education joyful and interesting.
- To explore the creative potential of the students.
- To create awareness about adolescent reproductive health among students, teachers and parents and developing healthy attitude towards sex and members of the opposite sex.
- Sensitize students towards gender issues.

Yuva Club : Each school shall constitute Yuva Club. The club shall organize competitions within school on singing, debates, elocution, quizzes, dance, painting, drama etc. The club shall organize competitions for talent hunt within the schools for both students and teachers. One teacher, preferable vocational guidance counselor, shall be incharge of that club. ₹ 10,000/- per school is being allocated for holding competition, in pursuit of developing creative potential among the students. In addition, each school organizes an exhibition on gender sensitivity and population education.

HIGHER EDUCATION

Every year thousands of foreign students from underdeveloped and developing countries come here for taking up higher education in Delhi. Subjects like Hindustani classical music, Animal husbandry, Buddhist studies, Agriculture, Indian Philosophy, Fine Arts, Veterinary Sciences, Sanskrit, Medical Science, Engineering, Law and other Indian Languages are taught in some of the best universities across the city. The city is a good educational destination for the students for it has some of the best institutions located here. Some of the leading institutions of the Capital are Netaji Subhas Institute of Technology, Lady Shri Ram College for Women, IIT Delhi, Delhi School of Economics, St Stephen's College, Indian Institute of Mass Communication, All India Institute of Medical Sciences (AIIMS), Delhi College of Engineering to name a few. The

Economic Survey of Delhi 2017-18 recorded 192 colleges in Delhi. In Delhi there are eleven deemed universities, one among which is an Open University. The top world renowned universities of Delhi are the Jawaharlal Nehru University, Delhi University, Jamia Millia Islamia, Jamia Hamdard, Guru Gobind Singh Indraprastha University and Indira Gandhi National Open University.

University of Delhi

The University of Delhi is a premier university of the country and is known for its high standards in teaching and research. Therefore, it attracts eminent scholars to its faculties. It was incorporated as a unitary teaching and residential university by an Act of Central Legislature in 1922. During those times, it had affiliated three arts colleges, viz, St. Stephen's College, Hindu College and Ramjas College, to its fold Lady Hardinge Medical College was affiliated to the Punjab University. The University, thus had a modest beginning with just three colleges, two faculties (Arts and Science) and about 750 students. The original conception of a unitary teaching university had to be given up gradually in favour of a federal university. Subject to the control and the coordinating influence of the university, the colleges remained autonomous teaching units, working in cooperation with one another and with the university. In 1933, the old Viceregal House was handed over by the government to the university, in 1941 colleges started shifting to the campus. Sir Maurice Gwyer, the Vice-Chancellor (1938-50), was the real architect of this University.

The Delhi University (Amendment) Act of 1952 made the University a teaching and an affiliating university and provision was made for the affiliation of colleges. Colleges were permitted outside the campus accordingly. The territorial jurisdiction of the University was originally limited to the area of ten miles radius from the Convocation Hall; now it extends to the entire area of Delhi. The following colleges and institutions are located in the campus: St. Stephen's College, Hindu College, Ramjas College, Indraprastha College, Sri Ram College of Commerce, Miranda House, Hans Raj College, Central Institute of

Education, Delhi School of Social Work, Kirori Mal College, SGTB Khalsa College, Vallabhbhai Patel Chest Institute and the Institute of Economic Growth. The South Campus made a beginning in 1973 by starting postgraduate programmes of some departments of the Faculty of Arts and Social Sciences in a rented building. The campus acquired land near Dhaula Kuan where the building of Arts Faculty was constructed and the offices and teaching activities shifted to this campus in 1983.

When the University Grants Commission (UGC) started establishing Centres of Advanced Studies in, the country during the early sixties, six such Centres were awarded to the University of Delhi out of a total of 18 centres. These Centres have been established for Physics, Chemistry, Botany, Zoology, Economics and Sociology. These Centres of Advanced Studies are now the Centres of Excellence in Teaching and Research in their respective areas. In addition, a number of these and other University departments received grants under the special assistance programme of the UGC for their outstanding academic work. The University has 15 libraries. These are apart from Libraries in the Colleges. The University Science Instrumentation Centre (USIC) has a number of sophisticated research instruments, which are used by several departments of the University, other institutions in Delhi and students from the neighbourhood.

Jamia Millia Islamia

Jamia Millia Islamia, a university of national repute, was established first at Aligarh and later, moved to Delhi. A staunch nationalist, Shaikhul Hind Maulana Mehmud Hasan, laid the foundation stone in Aligarh for Jamia Millia Islamia on October 29, 1920. In 1962, the institute was declared a deemed university and in 1988, it was declared a central university.

Guru Gobind Singh Indraprastha University

It is an affiliating and teaching University, established by Delhi government in 1998. Its focus is on professional education in emerging areas like engineering, technology, management studies, medicine, pharmacy, education etc. It has affiliated more than 50 institutes in Delhi and nearby areas to its fold. These affiliates have to run the programmes as per the norms and standards of the university.

Jawaharlal Nehru University

It is a central university, located in a 1000-acre campus in the Aravalli hill range. It was started during the early 1970s, opening doors for new disciplines and bringing new perspective to old disciplines. It has an excellent student-teacher ratio of 10:1. Only post-graduate courses are taken up in the JNU. Several centres in the university have been declared as the Centres of Excellence by the UGC. There are four special centres and 3 schools/centres that focus on frontline disciplines like Molecular Medicine, Information Technology and Law & Governance. Courses on Languages, Literature, Social Sciences and other inter-disciplinary subjects are also taught.

VOCATIONAL PROGRAMMES

Delhi introduced vocational programmes during the Seventh Five Year Plan. Important programmes are Steno (English and Hindi), Banking, Insurance, Textile Designing, Fashion Designing, Health Care and Beauty Culture, Medical Laboratory Technology, X-Ray Technology, Food Serving and Management, Electronics, Electrical Engineering, Computer Applications, Library Science, Tourism, Hotel Management, Bakery and Confectionary, Horticulture, Railway (commercial), Automobile Technology, Structure and Fabrication, Air Conditioning Technology etc. These vocational programmes were started because it was predicted that the bulk of the students would leave their academic streams and go for self-employment or gainful employment.

DISTANCE EDUCATION

Delhi Government runs Patrachar Vidyalaya for those students who cannot attend formal schools for various reasons. At the University level, the School of Correspondence Courses and Continuing Education was established by the Delhi University in July, 1962 to provide an efficient and less expensive method of education at the university level. It provides instructions through correspondence for the B.A. (Pass), B.Com, (Pass) and B.Sc. (General) courses. Nearly 85% of the total students enrolled in the correspondence courses are employed.

TECHNICAL EDUCATION

Delhi occupies a unique position in the arena of technical education. That is because of two reasons — firstly, its location is ideal and secondly, it has been a centre of activities, programmes, development and growth of technical education in the country for the last six decades. The establishment of Delhi Polytechnic (which later became Delhi College of Engineering) in 1942 played a pivotal role for the growth and development of technical education from the 1940s onwards. Delhi College of Engineering provided the initial impetus for setting up a number of national projects in higher technical education such as the premier IIT, Delhi in 1960, College of Pharmacy in 1964 and School of Planning and Architecture in 1964.

Engineering Courses—Government Institutions

- Delhi College of Engineering, Bawana Road
- Netaji Subhas Institute of Technology, Dwarka
- Mahila Institute of Technology, Kashmere Gate

Private Institutions (Affiliated to Guru Gobind Singh Indraprastha University)

- Maharaja Agrasen Institute of Technology, Sultanpuri
- Amity School of Engineering, Saket
- Guru Tegh Bahadur Institute of Technology, Tilak Nagar
- Bhartiya Vidya Peeth College of Engineering, Sector 13, Rohini

Privately Managed Institutes (offering AICTE—approved MBA/MCA/ PGDCA /PGDBM programmes)

- Institute of Business Administration & Management, Daryaganj
- Asia Pacific Institute of Management, Madanpur Khadar
- Apeejay School of Marketing, Tughlakabad Institutional Area
- Birla Institute of Management & Technology, Pushp Vihar
- Centre of Management Education, AIMA, AIMA House, Lodhi Road
- Entrepreneurship Management Process International, Mehrauli
- Fortune Institute of International Business, Krishna Farm, Bijwasan
- Guru Nanak Institute of Management, Punjabi Bagh
- Indian Institute of Finance, Ashok Vihar
- Institute of Integrated Learning in Management, Lodhi Inst. Area
- Jagan Institute of Management Studies, Pitampura
- Lal Bahadur Shastri Institute of Management, R. K. Puram

- Management Education & Research Institute, Vikaspuri
- New Delhi YMCA Institute of Management, Jai Singh Road
- Institute of Management, Tughlakabad Institutional Area
- Northern Institute of Integrated Learning in Management, Badarpur
- Rukmini Devi Institute of Management Studies, Pitampura
- Sardar Patel College of Communication & Management, K.G. Marg
- International Management Centre, NDSE-1
- Tecnia Institute of Advanced Studies, Sector-18, Rohini
- Institute of Management Science and Production Research, Jhandewalan Extension
- BLS Institute of Management, Barakhamba Road
- Vision School of Management Extension, New Delhi-37
- FORE School of Management, Shaheed Jeet Singh Marg
- Indraprastha Institute of Management, Sector-13, Rohini
- Delhi Institute of Advanced Studies, Sector-13, Rohini,
- Sri Sringeri Sharda Institute of Management, Vasant Vihar
- BV Institute of Management and Research, Janakpuri

Diploma Level—Govt. Institutions

- Ambedkar Polytechnic
- Arya Bhatt Polytechnic
- Govind Ballabh Pant Polytechnic
- Guru Nanak Dev Co-Educational Polytechnic
- Kasturba Polytechnic for Women
- Meera Bai Polytechnic for Women
- Pusa Polytechnic, PUSA
- Bhai Parmanand Institute of Business Studies

Government Sponsored Institutions

- Sharda Ukil School of Art
- Tool Room and Training Centre

Privately Managed Institutions

- Aditya Institute of Technology

- Baba Hari Das College of Pharmacy
- Sir Chhotu Ram Rural Institute of Engineering and Technology
- Father Agnel Polytechnic
- Guru Teg Bahadur Polytechnic
- International Polytechnic for Women
- Maharaja Surajmal Institute of Technology
- Marathwada Institute of Technology
- Rao Tula Ram Polytechnic
- Subramaniam Bharti College of Science & Technology

Indian Institute of Technology

It began as an engineering college in 1951. Later, in 1963, it was declared the Institute of Technology. Its object has been defined as "promotion of the highest standards in engineering."

School of Planning and Architecture

It was founded on October 16, 1959 after the integration of the Department of Architecture of the Delhi Polytechnic with the School of Town and Country Planning. This School offers B. Arch. and National Diploma Courses in Architecture.

Medical Education

There are quite a few medical colleges in Delhi. The Patel Chest Institute started the first diploma course in the field of tuberculosis in 1947 for training doctors in chest diseases, with a special emphasis on the fight against tuberculosis. It also aimed at conducting research on problems pertaining to all these diseases. The Institute specialises in Chemical Research, Pathology, Bacteriology, Bio-chemistry and Cardio-respiratory Physiology.

Lady Hardinge Medical College for Women was started in 1918 with only 34 students on the roll. Initially, it was to the Punjab University. Since 1950, the institution has been affiliated to the University of Delhi.

All India Institute of Medical Sciences was set up in 1956. It is an autonomous institution, which grants its own medical degrees, diplomas and other academic distinctions. It imparts medical education in all the branches so as to demonstrate a high standard of medical education before all the medical colleges and other allied institutions in India. This is a residential institution in which, all the faculty members, other staff and students live together.

Besides, MBBS degree courses are also conducted by Maulana Azad Medical College, University College of Medical Sciences and Vardhman Medical College. The Nehru Homeopathic College and Rajkumari Amrit Kaur College of Nursing are well-known in their respective fields. There are several other colleges, imparting education in Homeopathy, Unani Medicine, Ayurveda and Pharmacy.

Indian Agricultural Research Institute

It is recognised as the premier agricultural institute of the country where various problems of agricultural science are investigated. In 1958, the Institute received the status of the university for imparting postgraduate training in agricultural sciences and for granting the M.Sc. and Ph.D. degrees.

CULTURAL ORGANISATIONS

After the disappearance of the Mughal court, the interest in the cultivation of fine arts also declined. It was only after independence that an interest in cultural activities was revived. Now, there are many clubs, societies and institutions in Delhi for teaching music, dances, literature, painting and every kind of craft. Delhi, being the capital, has an advantage over other cities in the sence that the Government of India takes a keen interest in some cultural events for the distinguished visitors from abroad. Such events add glitter to the cultural life of the city. Many local authorities and people from different states coordinate and encourage literary and musical societies in their localities.

Sangeet Natak Academy

This National Academy of Music, Dance and Drama was set up in 1953 for the promotion of performing arts. It also extends financial help to traditional teachers and grants scholarships to students. The Academy is running a Kathak Kendra in New Delhi for imparting training in this classical form of dance. This Academy also honours outstanding performing artists and schools by conferring fellowships and annual awards on them.

Lalit Kala Academy

Set up in August, 1954, it promotes the study of painting, sculpture, architecture and applied arts through exhibitions, publications, a permanent symposium, seminars and lectures. It has also an artists' studio complex with facilities for training and practice in painting, ceramics etc.

Sahitya Akademi

Established in 1954, it is a national organisation to work actively for the development of Indian literature, set high literary standards, foster and coordinate literary activities in all the Indian languages and to promote the cultural unity of the country.

Indian Council for Cultural Relations

Established in 1950, it functions as an autonomous body and strives towards generating wider knowledge and more appreciation of the culture of India in other countries. It also acts to encourage the dissemination of knowledge and cultures of other countries in India.

Bhartiya Vidya Bhavan

Established in 1957, it aims at the re-integration of Indian culture with modern life and the resuscitation of its fundamental values. It runs public schools, an academy of foreign languages, a college of mass communications and a Sanskrit Department.

All India Fine Arts and Crafts Society

It was founded in 1928 for encouraging arts and stimulating greater public interest in India and abroad in Indian art and crafts. The Society conducts exhibitions, as well as it publishes art magazines and news bulletins. It also helps artists by arranging the sales of their works, art conferences and lectures.

Bhartiya Natya Academy

Set up in 1950, it has built an integral national theatre movement without any detriment to local traditions.

Sahitya Kala Parishad

Established in 1969 by Delhi Administration, it aims Indian literature and raising literary standards.

OTHER ORGANISATIONS

Some of the other prominent cultural bodies functioning in Delhi include: Gandharva Mahavidyalaya (culture, music); Triveni Kala Sangam (dance and music); Bhartiya Kala Kendra (culture and music); Delhi Musical Society (music); Punjab Kala Kendra, Kerala Kala Kendra (dance); Children's Little Theatre and The Little Theatre Group (dances and plays). The government also sponsored the establishment of the National School of Drama and the Children's Film Society. The College of Art was formerly the Art Department of the Delhi Polytechnic but in 1964, the Art Department was separated and became an independent College of Art, under Delhi Administration. The College imparts training in drawing and painting, sculpture and commercial art.

ORIENTAL INSTITUTIONS

Although, as compared with the nineteenth century, Oriental institutions are now losing their popularity, yet there are quite a few Arabic and Sanskrit institutions in Delhi where Arabic and Sanskrit are taught. Some of these institutions, which still survive, are Madrasa-i-Abdul Rab, Madrasa-i-Aminia, Madrasa-i-Alia, Fatehpuri, Madrasa Husain Baksh, Shri Ram Rishi Sanskrit Mahavidyalaya, the Mahavir Dal Sanskrit Pathshala (Dariba Kalan), Vishwanath Sanskrit Institution (Bela Road), Jhandewalan Sanskrit Pathshala and Shri Lal Bahadur Shastri Rashtriya Sanskrit Vidyapith. In the vicinity of the Jama Masjid, the Madrasa Riaz-ul-Uloom continues to give instructions in Hadith. Other notable Madrasas are Madrasa Siddiquia (Khari Baoli), Madrasa Ashrafia (Bazaar Machhliwalan), Madrasa Husainia Arabia Islamia, Madrasa Duaia (Sadar Bazaar) etc.

LIBRARIES

Presently, Delhi has many public, college and university libraries as well as those of other allied educational institutions, research bodies, cultural organisations and ministries. There are libraries of societies representing different states. Various embassies situated in Delhi have small and highly informative libraries such as the British Council Library and the USIS. Another factor for the growth of libraries has been the interest of people in Indian history and ancient institutions. Further, valuable records preserved in the National Archives of India Library and the rare acquisitions of the Archaeological Survey of India Library also attract attention of scholars and historians alike. Public libraries have also developed, viz, the library of the Indian Council for Cultural Relations, the American Library and the Max Muller Bhavan. The walled city of Delhi also houses some good public libraries such as the Hardinge (now Hardayal) Municipal Library, Delhi Public Library (which has branches all over Delhi), Mahavir Jain Library, Marwari Library and Shri Digambar Jain Library (in Chandni Chowk). The Central Secretariat Library of the Government of India, founded in 1951, is rich in official reports and publications. The library of the Indian Council of World Affairs, Sapru House, deals largely with contemporary history, particularly international law, international relations and the United Nations. The Delhi Public Library, has over 160000 volumes on its shelves; it also has a mobile van, which carries 2000 books to rural areas. Among the public libraries, Dayal Singh Library is also an important one, with good collection of books.

Transport

7

FROM the point of view of transport, Delhi is a centre of both national as well as international importance. Being the capital of the country and lying in the heartland of India, it has been receiving a continuous flow of people and goods since times immemorial. Its transport system has undergone massive changes and upgradation. The elephants, cavalry, chariots, camels, mules and bullocks are no longer used. The *dolis* and *palkis* have become things of the past and the use of tongas and *rehras* has been reduced to the minimum and that too, only in Old Delhi area.

BACKGROUND

Even during the olden days, Delhi had important road links with different parts of the country like Taxila in the north-west, Kurukshetra in the plains of Haryana, Hastinapur near Meerut and Kaushambi on the banks of Yamuna near Allahabad and Varanasi. There was active trade and commerce between Delhi and these towns. During the Sultanate period, when the capital city changed its sites several times, the massive and magnificent buildings constructed during those times bear evidences of beelike for transport activity that must have been necessitated the collection of materials and construction of these huge structures. Delhi occupied an important link on the Grand Trunk Road, which was built by Sher Shah Suri. It is a national highway of great importance now. During the Mughal era, Delhi enjoyed pivotal position in the network of roads with Agra-Delhi, Delhi-Lahore, Delhi-Ajmer and Delhi-Bareilly-Varanasi-Patna roads having the maximum traffics of passengers and traders. The transport system developed by the medieval rulers was made of much use by the East India Company during its early days. Lord William Bentinck took steps to have a permanent trunk road from Calcutta (now Kolkata) to Delhi and extend it to the north-western frontiers of those times.

PRESENT SCENE

The population of Delhi has been growing speedily and has increased from 9.4 million in 1990-1991 to 16.78 million in 2011. The total area of Delhi is 1483 sq. km with an urban area of about 1113.65 sq. km with high growth in transport demand over the years, congestion on roads has been increasing due to phenomenal rise in private transport. Concerted efforts have been made by the Government to increase transport mobility alongwith offering a better transport infrastructure. Transport was a priority sector in Eleventh Five Year Plan [2007-12] of Delhi. A single mode of public transport continued till 2002, when first corridor of Delhi Metro was started. Govt. of Delhi has planned to provide best multi modal public transport system to the citizens of Delhi which is based on a number of studies conducted so far.

ROAD NETWORK

The road network in Delhi is being developed and maintained by NHAI, PWD, MCD, NDMC, Delhi Cantonment Board and DDA. The road network in Delhi was 33,198 km (including 430 km of National Highways.

- **Sher Shah Suri Marg:** Earlier known as Grand Trunk Road (G.T. Road), it passes through the city and connects it to Punjab on one side and West Bengal on the other.

- **Mahatma Gandhi Marg:** Popularly known as Ring Road, it is a 48-km long circular road, encircling the middle part of the city. This 6-lane carriageway has a capacity of transporting 1.1 lakh vehicles per day. The government is making a number of flyovers on the road so as to make it free from red light stops. Through this road, one can reach any part of the city, at a fast pace and in a short time span.

- **Outer Ring Road:** This is another ring road, which encircles the peripheral parts of the town. However, now Delhi has spread even beyond the Outer Ring Road.

- **Mall Road:** An important road, it connects Old Delhi to the northern part of the town. Several offices of the Delhi Government are located along this road.

- **Parliament Street:** A very important road, it connects Parliament and Connaught Place. Several central government offices, banks and private offices are located along this road.

- **Rajpath:** It is a majestic road, leading from Rashtrapati Bhavan and Central Secretariat to India Gate; it is the most important road of Delhi central.

- **Janpath:** Most important among the roads, it connects the heart of New Delhi—the seat of power—with Connaught Place.

- **Netaji Subhash Chandra Bose Marg:** A thoroughfare, leading from Delhi Gate to the Jama Masjid crossing, it is now a busy and crowded market-place.

- **Ajmal Khan Road:** Delhi's busiest market is located along this road, in the Karol Bagh area.

- **Other Roads:** In Delhi, other important and famous roads are Kautilya Marg, Nyaya Marg, Aurobindo Marg, Akbar Road, Shahjahan Road, Shanti Path, Humayun Road, Ashoka Road, Pandara Road, Bahadur Shah Zafar Marg, Barakhamba Road, Kasturba Gandhi Marg, Baba Kharak Singh Marg, Jawahar Lal Nehru Road, Faiz Road, Mathura Road, Sham Nath Marg, G.T. Karnal Road, Rohtak Road, Desh Bandhu Gupta Road, Vikas Marg, Najafgarh Road, etc.

MODES OF CONVEYANCE

There are two types of vehicles, which are used by passengers in Delhi. One is the slow moving vehicles such as tongas, bicycles, rickshaws, *rehras* and animals for carrying goods and bullock-carts. Animals and animal-drawn carts are convenient vehicles for transporting goods and play an important role in the economy of Delhi. These carts generally belong to two principal categories–agricultural and industrial. Horse-driven carriages like tongas for passenger traffic are decreasing due to emergence of new and faster modes of conveyance on Delhi roads. Bicycle, on the other hand, is the most economical means of transport in Delhi. It is the common man's transport for his day-to-day life. Fast moving vehicles include motorcycles, auto-rickshaws, scooters, cars, trucks, vans, coaches, buses etc.

NATIONAL HIGHWAYS

Delhi has the distinction of having 5 National Highways passing through its territory. These are NH-1, NH-2, NH-8, NH-10 and NH-24 connecting National Capital Region of Delhi to rest of the country. These highways contribute significantly to the character of Delhi as a major trading and distribution center.

PERIPHERAL EXPRESSWAYS

Delhi has emerged as a major wholesale trade center for North India. It is estimated that 78% of vegetables and fruits, 49% of fuel, 44% of iron and steel and 47% of food grains traded in Delhi are destined for other States. The five national highways also bring interstate goods vehicles into the territory. This situation aggravates the traffic congestion, particularly on Ring Road, Outer Ring Road and other major roads of the city. As a solution to this problem, Western Peripheral Expressway and Eastern Peripheral Expressway project are being constructed.

WESTERN PERIPHERAL EXPRESSWAY

Total length of the road under western peripheral expressway is 135.65 kilo metre. It is being executed as single package on BOT basis and awarded to M/s. KPM Expressway Limited on 14th November, 2005 for a concession period of 23 years and 9 months (Including five years of construction).

EASTERN PERIPHERAL EXPRESSWAY

Total length of the road under this project is 135 kilo metre (90 km in Uttar Pradesh and 45 km in Haryana). Starts at Kundli NH-1 and terminate at Palwal on NH-2 via passing eastern peripheral of Delhi in Baghpat, Ghaziabad, Gautam Budh Nagar and Faridabad districts. The most of eastern peripheral expressway falls in Uttar Pradesh state and it is being implemented by the National Highway Authority of India (NHAI). The estimated cost of the project excluding the cost of land and shifting of utility services is ₹ 1885 crore.

INTER STATE BUS TERMINALS (ISBTs)

Master Plan of Delhi- 2021 suggested five ISBTs for Delhi. With the setting up of two new ISBTs at Sarai Kale Khan and Anand Vihar, three ISBTs are functioning at present. These three ISBTs cater to average 3.70-lakh passengers and 5235 buses/trips per day. Two more ISBTs are proposed to be constructed at Dwarka and Narela on BOT basis. Due to change in Floor Area Ratio (FAR) in Master Plan, 2021, there is a rethinking to take advantage of increased FAR and accordingly design and other parameters for construction of ISBTs are getting revised.

Signature Bridge: The existing bridge at Wazirabad is insufficient to meet the growing demands of large population of Trans Yamuna area especially Yamuna Vihar, Gokulpuri, Khajoori, Nand Nagri and the other areas. Therefore the GNCTD planned to construct Signature Bridge. It was inaugurated on Nov. 4, 2018.

Elevated Road Over Barapullah Nallah : The Phase-I of the project was completed before the Commonwealth Games and two clover leaves have also been completed during 2012-13. The second phase has been started in 2012-13. This project is covered under JNNURM. For parking facilities, MCD covered Kushak and Sunhari Bagh Nallah. Now Transport Department is utilizing this space for Bus Depots.

DELHI TRANSPORT INFRASTRUCTURE DEVELOPMENT CORPORATION

Government of Delhi has established Delhi Transport Infrastructure Development Corporation. The Corporation has been created with the objectives of development, implementation, operation and maintenance of urban transport infrastructure and funding of the expenses associated with transport planning, project development expenses for specific projects, capital expenditure support for specific projects and operations and maintenance expenditure for providing sustainable public services, external infrastructure for all ISBTs.

PRIVATE SECTOR CORPORATE BUS OPERATION SYSTEM

Government of Delhi decided to replace Blue Line Bus Operation System by Private Sector Corporate System. All Bus Routes have been merged into 17 clusters covering entire area of NCT of Delhi. Four clusters have been made operational with 300 buses. Five more clusters will be made operational very soon with about 1000 more new buses. Construction of new Bus Depots is being expedited so as to provide parking and workshop space to private sector corporate for new clusters to be covered.

PUBLIC TRANSPORT

In Delhi, the public transport system is one of the major transport systems and hence, its problems are manifold. The travel demand in Delhi has increased rapidly. More people need to commute as a result of sharp rise in its population. Mobility has increased because of the changes in the socio-economic characteristics of the tripmakers and more opportunities offered by the city. A large number of informal commercial establishments further encourage people to travel over longer distances to their places of work. With an increase in the size and area of the city, trip lengths increased and the burden of commuter travel was transferred public transport. In addition to the residents of Delhi, people travel from far flung places for getting employment. The length of roads in Delhi was 8231 km in 1970-71, which increased sharply to 33,198 km. by 2017-18.

Public transport in Delhi has two major components viz. bus transport and metro rail. These two major transport systems are playing a vital role in facilitating public transport in Delhi. In fact, both the systems are the lifeline of the people of Delhi. At present, the daily ridership of Delhi Metro is 25 lakh. Ridership on Metro Rail is further expected to increase after completion of the final stage of construction of DMRC's Phase-III, additional corridors and NCR extensions. However, daily average passenger ridership on DTC and cluster buses is 43 lakh. Total 252 Km length of Metro line was completed under Phase-I, Phase-II and Phase-III in Delhi by 31.03.2018 and 327 km metro line is operational up to 31.12.2018. Another about 23 KM of Metro rail of Phase III including additional corridors with NCR extensions, being implemented concurrently, are expected to be opened by 2020 in stages.

VEHICULAR TRAFFIC

The number of vehicles, particularly that of motorized vehicles, has increased from just 204078 in 1971 to about 109.86 lakh in March 2018. Interestingly, at present, the number of all types of vehicles in Delhi is more than the total number of vehicles in Mumbai, Kolkata and Chennai put together. The number of non-motorized vehicles has also increased. In fact, the human population has doubled during the past two decades but the number of vehicles has increased fifteen-fold during these two decades. On the other hand, development of road network has been marginal but the number of vehicles has grown enormously, this resulting in more vehicles per 100 kms. of road length. The result is an extreme congestion on all the roads, slow speeds, an increase in road accidents, fuel wastage and environmental pollution, with motorized vehicles alone contributing to about two-third of the atmospheric pollution.

The growth rate of vehicles in Delhi during 1999-2012 was recorded at 135.59 per cent while average annual compound growth rate at 6.81 per cent. The highest growth of vehicles during the period was observed in taxies at 707 per cent, other passenger vehicles and car & jeeps stand second and third positions at 313 per cent and 168 per cent respectively. The negative growth of vehicles recorded in others row which is due to the inclusion of all goods vehicles in the separate rows.

HISTORY OF DTC

It was in 1935 that a public limited company, called Gwalior Northern India Transport Company Limited, was established for giving licenses to operate buses in Delhi. After independence, this bus service was nationalized in 1948, under the direct control of the Delhi Transport  Service of the Union Ministry of Surface Transport. The transport scenario in the capital was initially streamlined by constituting Delhi Transport Undertaking in 1950. It became an undertaking of the Municipal Corporation of Delhi by an Act of Parliament in April,1958. The Working Group of Planning Commission concluded that Delhi Transport, as an extension of Municipal Corporation of Delhi, had not been functioning efficiently and adequately, thus resulting in a loss of revenues and very high operational costs. On the recommendation of the Commission, the Government of India took over the management of the undertaking, its assets and liabilities.

Thus, the Delhi Transport Corporation was set up in 1971, with the objective of providing or promoting an efficient, economical, reliable and properly coordinated system of road transport in Delhi and around it. In doing so, it was supposed to act on sound business principles so as to achieve a high-level operational efficiency and attain financial self-sufficiency. The DTC, which was functioning under the administrative control of Government of India, was finally taken over by Government of the NCT Delhi on August 5, 1996.

Delhi Transport Corporation has been consistently incurring financial losses. Financial mismanagement has been the hallmark of the DTC since its inception. The Corporation funds its operations through government loans but incurs losses on operations, including social costs such as money waived to students as concessional bus passes. This financial crisis has deepened due to its buses plying on unprofitable routes, lower utilization of assets, higher operational costs and a stagnant pricing framework. Operational efficiency is affected because the Corporation has to serve colonies located far and wide in the metropolis. Furthermore, it has been over-staffed to the hilt.

In 1991, the Delhi Transport Corporation had 2500 buses; this number came down to 1500 in 1995. Further, the fleet was reduced to 1000 buses by the end of 1996. However, new buses were required to replace the ageing DTC fleet and also, to meet the demands of increased number of commuters. Government did not have that kind of capital. During the last few years, efforts have been made to develop a range of privatised bus services. Based on a combination of fare structure and stoppage between specific points, the Delhi transport scene has acquired many hues. Privatised services comprised the Red Line, White Line and Blue Line buses. Later, however, most of the Red Line buses were painted blue-and-white, as they had lost their credibility. Privatisation, however, gave birth to its own unique problems. For example, routes of 900 buses were changed to more profitable ones, without any reference to operating costs. This adversely affected other routes and the convenience of the commuters. Further, the State Transport Authority did not look into the parking needs of the private bus operators. This led to the parking of the Red Line buses all over the residential areas of the city.

DTC is responsible for providing efficient public transport services to the people of Delhi at affordable prices. DTC was handed over to the Government of NCT of Delhi by the Government of India in August 1996. The performance of DTC during 2001-17 is presented in Statement given on the next page:

Performance of Delhi Transport Corporation

Sl. No.	Years	Fleet (No)	Fleet Utilization (%)	Passenger carried (million)
1.	2008-09	3804	77.03	772
2.	2009-10	4725	80.99	776
3.	2010-11	6204	75.03	700
4.	2011-12	5892	84.27	863
5.	2012-13	5445	85.77	973
6.	2013-14	5223	85.51	952
7.	2014-15	4712	83.99	930
9.	2015-16	4352	83.63	927
10.	2016-17	4027	85.12	890

Source : Operational Statistics of DTC

CNG ISSUE

Indraprastha Gas Limited, a joint venture of the Gas Authority of India Ltd. and the Delhi Government, was started in 1998 to provide Compressed Natural Gas (CNG) to Delhi as a fuel. The process was started as a trial but gained much momentum after the Supreme Court made it mandatory for the public transport vehicles of Delhi to use CNG. Initially, there was an acute shortage of CNG but after the commissioning of pumping stations, the supply became satisfactory. Almost 90 CNG stations are working in Delhi.

RAIL NETWORK

Delhi is a major junction on the rail map of India linked with all the major metropolitan cities directly. There are four main railway stations viz. at New Delhi, Old Delhi, Hazrat Nizamuddin and Sarai Rohila, besides Container Depots at Patparganj and Tuglakabad. A new Railway Station has been developed by Northern Railway at Anand Vihar, which would help in decongestion at New Delhi and Old Delhi Railway Stations. New Delhi Railway Station has been renovated, expanded and provided with better facilities for commuters. Renovation of Delhi Railway Station is in progress. Renovation and expansion of Nizamuddin railway Station is likely to start shortly.

MASS RAPID TRANSIT SYSTEM (MRTS)

MRTS PHASE-1 (65.05 KM) : The Mass Rapid Transit System (MRTS) is an ambitious project that aims at providing a non-polluting and efficient rail-based transport system, properly integrated with the road transport system. The first phase of the project, originally estimated to cost ₹ 4,860 crore (April 1996 prices) was approved in September 1996 and was to be completed by March, 2005. Later on it was revised to be completed by March 2006 with an estimated cost of ₹ 10571 crore. Dwarka Sub-city corridor has been implemented with the additional funding of ₹320 crore by Delhi Development Authority (DDA).

PLAN OF FIRST PHASE OF MRTS

SI. No.	Name of Section	Length (km)
1.	Delhi University – Central Secretariat (Underground Corridor)	11
2.	Shahdara – Rithala (Rail/surface/elevated Corridor)	22.06
3.	Indraprastha – Barakhamba Road, Dwarka (Underground/ elevated Corridor)	25.65
4.	Dwarka sub-city (Dwarka – Dwarka Sector VI)	6.50
	Total	**65.05**

COMMISSIONING OF FIRST PHASE OF MRTS

SI. No.	Corridor	Name of the Section	Length (Km)	Commissioned on
1.	Line 1	Shahdara-Tis Hazari	8.40	25.12.2002
		Tis Hazari-Inderlok	4.90	04.10.2003
		Inderlok-Rithala	8.70	31.03.2004
2.	Line 2	Vishwa Vidhyalaya - Kashmere Gate	4.00	20.12.2004
		Kashmere Gate - Central Secretariat	7.00	03.07.2005
3.	Line 3	Barakhamba - Dwarka	22.90	31.12.2005
		Brakhambha - Indraprastha	2.70	11.11.2006
		Dwarka Sub-City	6.50	01.04.2006

In Delhi, the Metro Trains run from 6.00 AM in the morning till about 11.00 PM in the night. The train frequency varies from 3 minutes a peak time upto 12 minutes in non-peak hours. The expected ridership is 21.82 lakh passengers per day for MRTS network.

MRTS PHASE-II: After completion of MRTS Phase-I, the work of Phase-II has also been completed. The information regarding corridors of MRTS Phase-II is presented below:

CORRIDORS PROPOSED/COMMISSIONED DURING MRTS PHASE-II

Sl. No.	Corridor	Name of the Section	Length (Km)	Target Date	Date of Operation
1.	Line 1 Extn	Shahdara – Dilshad Garden	3.09	Dec. 2008	04.06.2008
2.	Line 2 Extn	Vishwa Vidhyalaya – Jahangir Puri	6.36	Oct. 2009	04.02.2009
		Central Secretariat – Qutub Minar	11.76	Aug. 2010	03.09.2010
		Qutub Minar – Huda City Center Gurgaon	15.82	June 2010	21.06.2010
3.	Line 3 Extn	Indraprastha – Yamuna Bank	2.17	J une 2009	10.05.2009
		Yamuna Bank – New Ashok Nagar	5.90	Nov. 2009	13.11.2009
		New Ashok Nagar – Noida City Center	7.00	Nov. 2009	13.11.2009
4.	Line 4	Yamuna Bank – Anand Vihar	6.17	Dec. 2009	07.01.2010
5.	Line 5	Inderlok – Mundka	15.15	Mar. 2010	02.04.2010
		Kirti Nagar–Ashok Park	3.31	Dec. 2010	27.08.2011
6.	Line 6	Central Secretariat – Sarita Vihar	15.34	Sep. 2010	03.10.2010
		Sarita Vihar – Badarpur	4.82	Nov. 2010	14.01.2011

Sl. No.	Corridor	Name of the Section	Length (Km)	Target Date	Date of Operation
7.	PPP Line	High Speed Airport Metro Express Line – New Delhi Railway Station to Dwarka Sector-21	22.7	Nov. 2010	23.02.2011

The total length of MRTS Phase II is 122.36 KM and total completion cost (for Gurgaon Extn. Cost of Delhi portion only considered) is estimated at ₹ 19,231.36 Crore including concessionaire contribution off ₹ 1786.40 Crore. Extension of Delhi Metro in Dwarka Sub-city from Dwarka Sectors 9 to 21 for a length of 2.77 km has been completed as deposit work of DDA. The line is operational from 30.10.2010.

PHYSICAL INFRASTRUCTURE-RAILWAYS-DMRC

Phase-III Network	
Line	**Length (km)**
Line-7-Majlis Park-Shiv Nagar	58.59
Line-8-Janakpuri West-Kalindi Kunj	34.27
Line-6-Central Secretariat-Kashmiri Gate	9.37
Line 2 Extn.-Jahangirpuri-Badli	4.48
Line 6 S-Badarpur-Faridabad	13.87
Line 5 Extn.-Mundka-Bahadurgarh	11.18
Dwarka-Najafgarh	2.75
Kalindikunj-Botanical garden	3.96
Escorts Mujesar-Ballabhgarh	3.20
Dilshad Garden-Ghaziabad Bus Adda	9.41
Noida City Centre-Sector 62 Noida	6.67
Phase-IV Network (Proposed)	
6 Corridors	103.93

Phase IV is still currently in the proposal phase was originally planned to start construction in 2016 and had a 2021 deadline. However delays in approval have delayed the completion deadline to at least 2023. In June 2016, the Detailed Project Report (DPR) for the Phase IV was approved. In January 2017, the Delhi Government approved the Phase IV plan. In July 2017, the Delhi cabinet granted the final approval to the INR 50,000 crore plan in July 2017 on a 50:50 equity basis with the Union Government. In June 2017, the Government of Haryana's cabinet approved the investment of INR 968.20 crore as its share on the 80:20 equity ratio with the union Government, for the 4.86 kilometres (3.02 mi) extension of Delhi Metro from the existing Rithala metro station to Sonipat via Bawana with three elevated stations at Sector 5 of Narela in Delhi, on Delhi border at Kundli Industrial Area and Nathupur Industrial Area in Sonipat, which are planned to be built as part of Phase IV. In 2018, a report by the Delhi Government's finance department has criticized a number of corridors in Phase IV as not economically sustainable and lack sufficient ridership to justify the cost of construction. The department singled out the new Tughlakabad – Aerocity and Inderlok – Indraprastha Lines and the north extension of the Red Line to Narela and Sonipat as not economically viable.

AIR TRANSPORT

Delhi being the capital of the country, is well connected by air lines to different parts of the country and the world. The Imperial Airways made its inaugural flight from Cairo and arrived at Delhi on January 8, 1927. Thereafter, a weekly flight was operated by Imperial Airways with effect from December 30, 1929. The air station at New Delhi was set up in 1927 and in 1928, flying club was set up at Delhi. The first administrative building of the airport was constructed at the New Delhi aerodrome, called Safdarjung Airport. The Airport has a runway of 3500 ft. which is inadequate for modern types of planes. It is now being used only by the Indian Airlines' smaller aircraft and private planes and gliders of the Delhi Flying Club and Delhi Gliding Club for training purpose. Palam Air Port was constructed during World War II. The Airport has a runway of 12500 ft. to meet the requirement of aircraft like Boeing 747. Now, it is being used for domestic flights only. The Indira Gandhi International Airport (Terminal-I) is used for domestic flights whereas the Indira Gandhi International Airport (Terminal-II) serves as an important international airport, linking the city with different parts of the world. A large number of international air companies, apart from Air India, use this airport. The control of these airports is done by Airports Authority of India.

❏ ❏ ❏

8 Communication

DELHI has the modern communication network, commensurate with its status as the capital of the nation and Metropolitan city. All means of communication—like postal, telecommunication, satellite and others — are available.

Delhi's telephone system was established in Delhi in 1911, with a manual exchange. The first automatic exchange was opened in 1926 and the first manual trunk exchange was opened in 1945. In 1964, the telephone capacity in Delhi went past 50000. Eight years later, this capacity crossed the 1-lakh mark. In 1977, the STD service was launched, with connections to Ambala and Indore. In 1984, the first telex exchange was opened while radio paging service was started in 1985. In 1986, a corporate entity, the Mahanagar Telephone Nigam Ltd. (MTNL) took over the operations of Delhi and in the same year, the first digital exchange was started in Rajouri Garden. The mid-1990s saw major developments in this direction, with the introduction of paging, mobile, Internet and IT related services. The basic telephone service (in Delhi) is provided by the MTNL and Bharati Telenet which was (started in 2001).

Cellular services are provided by Bharati (under the brand name Airtel), Tata Teleservices (brand name Tata), MTNL (under the brand name Dolphin), Relience (Under the brand name Jio) and Vodafone. All these companies provide pre-paid cash cards as well as SIM cards. They also provide a number of value-added services like voice-mail, SMS etc.

COMMUNICATION IN INDIA & DELHI

S.No.	Mode of Communication Facilities	India		Per cent	
		2001	2011	2001	2011
1.	Radio/Transistor	35.10	19.90	50.00	33.40
2.	Television	31.60	47.20	74.50	88.00
3.	Telephone	9.10	63.20	34.70	90.80
4.	None of the Specified Mode of Communication	50.40	27.40	18.20	3.5

Source: Census of India, 2011, Houses, Household Amentities and Assets.

❐ ❐ ❐

Delhi was among the first cities in India to enjoy the electricity which was supplied to its citizens which even prior to its elevation to the status of the capital of India in 1911. All the urban and rural areas in Delhi have been electrified.

Delhi being a city state with diminishing rural areas and agricultural activities, the thrust on energy front in Delhi is mainly to have uninterrupted power supply and to take care of increasing power demand. Government of Delhi introduced power sector reforms during the beginning of the 10th Five Year Plan with the corporatisation of transmission and generation and privatization of distribution of power. This has dramatically changed the power scenario of Delhi as the transmission and distribution loss, which was responsible for negative returns in this sector, has been significantly reduced.

BACKGROUND

The John Flaming Company was granted license by the government in 1905 to engage in the business of electricity supply in Delhi by establishing a small diesel generating station near Lahori Gate. This undertaking was purchased in 1908 by a British Company, called Delhi Tramway and Lighting Company. It later changed its name to the Delhi Electric Supply and Traction Company Limited. In order to meet the capital's requirement of electricity, the Government of India installed a steam generating station at Kingsway Camp. Later, the power station was shifted to Rajghat and called Central Power House.

The Delhi State Electricity Board was established in March, 1951. In the beginning of the First Five Year Plan, the Delhi State Electricity Board, New Delhi Municipal Committee and Upper Yamuna Valley Electricity Supply Company were the three organisations that were distributing and supplying electricity in Delhi, New Delhi and Shahdara areas respectively. With the formation of the Municipal Corporation on

April, 7, 1958, the Delhi State Electricity Board stood dissolved and its functions were taken over by Municipal Corporation of Delhi, which performed these functions through the Delhi Electric Supply Undertaking (DESU). The functions of the Yamuna Valley Electric Supply Undertaking were also taken over by DESU. The DESU also supplied bulk power to New Delhi Municipal Council, the distribution licensee for the area.

From 1st July, 2002 under the Delhi Electricity Reforms Act, DVB was unbundled into Six companies comprising of a Generation Company, a Transmission Company, three distribution companies and one holding company. The Generation and Transmission functions are performed by the two companies, i.e., Genco and Transco as wholly State Government owned companies, the distribution functions have been entrusted to two private companies viz BSES and TATA Power Ltd. BSES has taken up two distribution companies namely; BSES Rajdhani Power Ltd. and BSES Yamuna Power Ltd., while the third company is with TATA Power which has been named as New Delhi Power Ltd. Transco company also makes available bulk supply of power to NDMC and MES for distribution in their respective areas.

POWER GENERATION

While demand has been growing rapidly, capacity addition has remained relatively stagnant. Delhi's total installed generation capacity is 8,346.72 MW. Nearly 28% of Delhi's power needs are met by its own plants and BTPS and remaining 72% by import from NTPC and other sources.

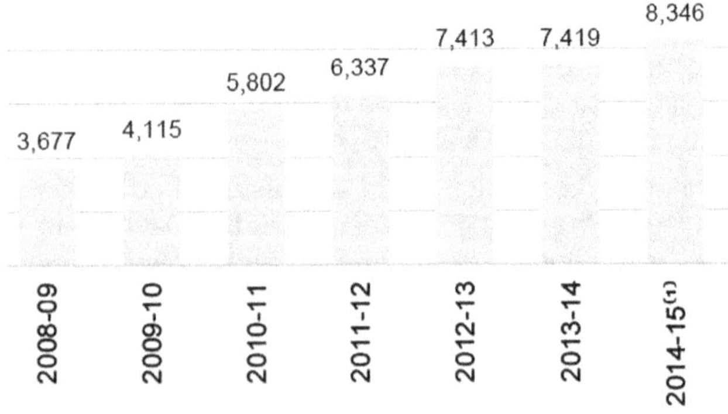

The power generation in Delhi is undertaken by two Govt. owned companies, *i.e.*, Indraprastha Power Generation Co. Ltd. (IPPGCL) and Pragati Power Corporation Ltd. (PPCL). IPPGCL owned three plants, *i.e.*, Rajghat Power House, I.P. Power Station and GTPS. Of these GTPS and Pragati Power Stations are gas based and the other two are coal.

POWER DISTRIBUTION

Delhi has a total consumer base of 55.68 lakh, electricity to whom is being supplied by 5 Licensees, 3 private distribution Companies (BRPL, BYPL, NDPL), NDMC and MES.

RENEWABLE ENERGY

For mass scale adoption of solar energy as green power in Delhi, a Policy named as "Delhi Solar Policy-2016" has been notified on 27.09.2016. Delhi Govt. formed Energy Efficiency and Renewal Energy Management Centre (EE&REMC) to work as 'State Designated Agency (SDA)' to coordinate, regulate and enforce Energy Conservation Act, 2001 in Delhi in association with Bureau of Energy Efficiency (BEE).

POWER IN DELHI : At a Glance

- The supply of electricity in Delhi periphery increased from 37484 million units in 2014-15 to 38510 million units in 2017-18.
- The total number of electricity consumers in Delhi are 57.55 lakh in 2017-18. Number of electricity consumers in Delhi have increase by 71.92% during the last ten years.
- The total power purchase in Delhi has grown by 55.38% during the last ten years.
- Peak demand increased from 5925 MW in 2014-15 to 6526 MW in 2017-18.
- Aggregate Technical & Commercial (AT&C) losses in Delhi reduced significantly from 52% in the pre-reform era to 9.41% in 2017-18.
- A new scheme, namely, "Mukhyamantri Agriculture-cum-Solar Farm Scheme" has been approved to promote and increase solar power generation.
- The total installed capacity of renewable energy in Delhi is 170.35 MW (Solar 118.35 MW + Waste to energy 52 MW) as on 31.12.2018.

❏ ❏ ❏

10 Water Supply

WATER supply and sewerage are an essential component of the basic infrastructure for urban settlement. The number of house holds in Delhi has increased from 18.61 lakh in March 1991 to about 34.41 lakh in March 2011.

As per 2011 census, 33.41 lakh households were in Delhi, out of which 27.16 lakh households were provided piped water supply system. About 4.61 lakh households were getting water supply through tube wells/deep bore hand pumps/public hydrants and remaining 1.64 lakh households depended on other sources like river, canal, ponds, tank, spring, etc.

Water supply and treatment capacity is being increased in Delhi almost in each five year plan taking into account the requirement of drinking water for the population increasing at a very high rate, almost more than double to the rate of increase at national level. In spite of best efforts made by the Government, water supply in an equitable and or adequate way remained a matter of concern due to various reasons like raw water scarcity and related problems, transmission and distribution losses, supply with less pressure, uneven distribution, depleting ground water level, nonrecharge of ground water due to rapid urbanization, increasing cost of water treatment and increasing gap between water supply cost and tariff, etc.

BACKGROUND

The main source of water supply in Delhi during the olden days was shallow wells. These wells were found to be inadequate and untenable on sanitary grounds. Many wells used to go dry during the summers. In 1889, several wells were dug up near Chandrawal and water was supplied through a reservoir built at the Ridge. Later, due to the construction of New Delhi and Cantonment, this system was changed to direct withdrawal of raw water from the river Yamuna at Wazirabad; it was carried by gravity through masonry conduits to Chandrawal for treatment by sand filters. In 1926, the Delhi Joint Water and Sewage Agency was set up for efficient supply of water and also, for quick sewage disposal. With an increase in the populations of Delhi and New Delhi, water works at Wazirabad and Chandrawal were expanded to cope with the surge in water demand. A barrage was constructed in 1959 across the river Yamuna near Wazirabad to store water. Additional intake works and an treatment plant were also constructed at Okhla. Rain wells were dug in Shahdara and tubewells in South Delhi and West Delhi to augment the supply of water the city.

Water Treatment Plants: 2016 & 2018

S.No.	Name of Plant	Capacity (MGD)	
		2016	2018
1.	Chandrawal Water House No. 1 & II	90	90
2.	Wazirabad I, II & III	120	120
3.	Haiderpur	200	200
4.	North Shahdara (Bhagirathi)	100	100
5.	Bawana	20	20
6.	Nangloi	40	40
7.	Sonia Vihar	140	140
8.	Ranney Wells and Tube Wells	80	80
9.	Recycling of Waste Water at, Bhagirathi, Haiderpur and Wazirabad	45	45
10.	Commonwealth Games Village	01	01
11.	Okhla	20	20
12.	Dwarka	50	50
	Total	906	906

WATER RESOURCES

The water resources of DJB are given below: (March 2018)

Source of Water	Quantity (MGD)
Yamuna River	375
Ganga River	240
Bhakra Storage	218
Ground Water / Ranney Well/Tube Well	80
Total	913

The decreasing ground water level in Delhi has become a matter of serious concern. At some places in South and South-West Delhi, the water level has gone 20-30 meter below the ground level. The quality of underground water is deteriorating in several places. It has been found to be unfit for human consumption. The salinity of ground water is increasing in South-West and North-West Delhi. In some areas of Shahdara and Kanjhawala, Nitrate content has been found to be more than 1000 mg/liter. Fluoride and chemical concentrations, more than prescribed limits, have also been found in ground water at various locations in Delhi. To tackle these problems, the Central Ground Water Board has taken steps to regulate the number of tube-wells being commissioned in Delhi.

PARALLEL CHANNEL FROM MUNAK TO HAIDERPUR

About 30-50 per cent of the raw water discharged from Tajewala Head-works is lost in the present water carrier system through the Yamuna River and the Western Yamuna Canal system. To prevent this loss, a parallel pucca channel is under construction from Munak to Haiderpur. This channel of 102 kms. Length is being constructed by the Haryana Government. The estimated cost is ₹ 525 crore. The entire cost of the project will be financed by Delhi Government. Water availability will increase by 80 MGD on construction of this channel. A stretch of around only 250 meter has not been completed by Haryana Government inspite of repeated requests at all levels.

RAIN WATER HARVESTING

DJB has provided Rain Water Harvesting in its 151 no. installations. DJB has provided financial assistance to the tune of ₹ 82 lakh for 172 cases in the institutional category for providing Rain Water Harvesting Systems. The Rain Water Harvesting Cell of DJB provides technical assistance to individuals for providing Rain Water Harvesting. DJB has provided the information regarding Rain Water Harvesting on its website for public facilitation. 2 no. of NGOs have been engaged by DJB to create public awareness and promote community participation to implement Rain Water Harvesting.

Industrial Development   11

INDUSTRIALISATION has the potential to achieve a variety of economic and social objectives such as employment, poverty eradication, gender equality, labour standards, and greater access to education and healthcare. At the same time, industrial processes can have negative environmental impacts, causing climate change, loss of natural resources, air and water pollution and extinction of species. These threaten the global environment as well as economic and social welfare.

SIXTH ECONOMIC CENSUS

As per the Sixth Economic Census there were 8.75 lakhs establishments working in Delhi during 2013, as compared to 7.58 lakhs establishments in 2005 at the time of the fifth Economic Census, registering an annual growth of 1.94%. Also, out of 8.75 lakhs enterprises, only 12,441 (1.4%) were in the rural area and 8.63 lakhs (98.6%) were operated in the urban area. Out of 8.75 lakhs establishments, around 7.96 lakhs (91%) establishments were under private proprietorship, while around 4.70 lakhs (53.7%) worked outside household with fixed structure and remaining 4.05 lakhs (46.3%) were operated outside household without fixed structure of inside household. Nearly 30.2 lakhs people (27,610) in rural areas and 29.9 lakhs in urban area) were working in 8.75 lakh establishments in Delhi during 2013 with an average of 3.45 people per establishment—out of 30.2 lakhs, about 3.8 lakhs (12.5%) were female and 26.4 lakhs (87.5%) were male workers.

The maximum number i.e. 3.7 lakh establishments (42.3%) were engaged in trade, followed by 1.56 lakhs (17.8%) in manufacturing activity, 72,572 (8.3%) in transportation and storage and 48,051(5.5%) in accommodation and food service activities. On the other hand, the manufacturing sector engaged a maximum number of 10 lakhs (33.2%)

people, followded by 8.6 lakhs (28.4%) in trade and 1.8 lakhs (5.9%) in transportation and storage. For the first time the information on handicraft and handloom establishments was collected in Sixth Economic Census — the total number of handicraft/handloom establishments has been reported as 9,260 with 35,553 people engaged (an average of 3.8 workers per establishment).

OPERATION AND MAINTENANCE OF INDUSTRIAL ESTATES UNDER PPP MODEL

In order to maximise efficiency with the available resources, the Government has decided to develop and maintain industrial infrastructure on Public Private Partnehip basis. Four industrial estates namely Okhla, Patparganj, Bawana and Narela have been selected as pilot project for maintenance of industrial estates on PPP model under a BOT concession to a private partner for 15 years.

BUSINESS FACILITATION COUNCIL (BFC)

Issues pertaining to the industry sector. e.g., Grant of consent to establish/ operate an industrial unit, grant of factory licence at all floors in industrial use premises, sanctioning of building plan, guidelines for redevelopment of approved industrial areas etc. have been resolved. The Council is also acting as a hand holding agency to guide existing units into becoming technologically more advanced, less polluting and moving to knowledge based or high-technology activity.

INDUSTRIAL POLICY

The first industrial policy for Delhi was published in 1982. Following the rapid urbanization in Delhi combined with demographic transition and environmental consequences and emergence of Information Technology Enabled Services, a new Industrial Policy was required to be put in place to take care of the said changes. Accordingly a new Industrial Policy was announced in 2010. The objectives of the industrial policy, 2010 are to

- Promote non-polluting and clean industries.
- Promote high technology and skilled industries in Delhi to keep in-migration of unskilled worker to a minimum level.
- Develop world class infrastructure within planned industrial estates and regularized industrial clusters.

- Promote cluster approach and walk to work concepts wherever possible.
- Facilitate business through procedural simplifications and e-governance measures.
- Promote transparent and business friendly environment.

The vision to make Delhi a hub of clean, high-technology and skilled economic activities by 2021 by policy shift essential to change industrial profile from low-skilled to high tech and high skilled by adopting the following strategy:

- Infrastructure Development through better Operation and Maintenance of industrial assets.
- Facilitating business by simplification and e-enabling measures.
- Support skill development and other promotional measures like allowing Knowledge based Industries in industrial area among others.
- Decongesting industrial areas through redevelopment schemes.
- Promoting cluster development of high-technology and skilled industries in new industrial areas through public private partnerships.
- Discourage polluting industries through higher infrastructure development fee.

KNOWLEDGE BASED INDUSTRIAL PARK AT BAPROLA

DSIIDC is developing Knowledge Based Industrial Park at Baprola in an area of approximately 55 acres. The estimated project cost is about ₹ 2575 crore. The project will cater to the specific needs of Information Technology, ITeS Industry, Media, Research & Development, Gems & Jewellery and other business services. The project is expected to provide direct employment to about 01 lakh persons and indirect employment to about 1.70 lakh persons.

Industrial buildings are proposed to be developed as green building with the target of four star GRIHA rating. All industrial and commercial buildings shall be centrally air condition.

Development of a new industrial area at Kanjhawala

DSIIDC intends to develop an integrated industrial township at Kanjhawala. The proposed project shall be major Greenfield Project spread over in an area of 920 acres. The project will spearhead the industrialization of North West Delhi and also create vast employment opportunities for people directly and indirectly.

DELHI FINANCIAL CORPORATION

The Delhi Financial Corporation (DFC) caters to the financial needs of industries located in the National Capital Territory of Delhi and the Union Territory of Chandigarh.

Financial assistance is available to the industrial as well as service sectors units like medical and health care/diagnostic centers, transport sector, hotels, restaurants. Tourism related facilities like amusement parks, convention centers, software/hardware services relating to information technology, telecommunication or electronics including satellite, linkage, Audio/Video/Visual communication, Hi-tech Agro Industries, floriculture, Tissue culture, aqua pollutary farming, breeding hatcheries etc. The upper limit for grant of loans in case of companies and co-operative Societies is ₹ 10 crore while for proprietorship and partnership firms it is ₹ 4 crore. The loans are available to new industrial units as well as existing ones for shifting, expansion, modernization, diversification and rehabilitation. Loans are also provided to the units for upgradation of technology resulting in less consumption of power and increase in qualitative productivity as also pollution control equipment etc. DFC is also providing loans to small road transport operators for commercial vehicles. In order to make Delhi an environment friendly city, DFC facilitated the relocation process of industrial units by providing loans on concessional terms.

DELHI STATE INDUSTRIAL & INFRASTRUCTURE DEVELOPMENT CORPORATION LTD.

DSIIDC was incorporated as a company and registered under Companies Act, 1956 in February, 1971 with the main objects of aiding, counselling, assisting, financing, projecting and promoting the interests of small industries in Delhi and providing them with capital, credit, resources and technical and managerial assistance for the successful execution of their work and business. At the time of registration it was known as Delhi Small Industries Development Corporation Limited. However, now it is called **'Delhi State Industrial & Infrastructure Development Corporation Limited'**.

DELHI KHADI & VILLAGE INDUSTRIES BOARD

Delhi Khadi & Village Industries Board was constituted in the year 1983 under Himachal Pradesh Khadi and Village Industries Board Act as extended to Delhi. At present the Board is implementing Rural Employment Generation Programme (Margin Money) scheme in Delhi. The scheme is owned by Khadi and Village Industries Commission, Govt. of India and implemented by this Board in the rural areas of NCT of Delhi through the nationalized banks.

❑ ❑ ❑

Trade & Commerce 12

TRADE and commerce have played a pivotal role in shaping the development of Delhi's economy by making a significant contribution in terms of tax revenues and providing gainful employment. Delhi is the biggest trade and consumption centre in North India. Delhi distinguishes itself as a centre for entrepot trade which means that large part of its economic activity is concerned with the redistribution of goods produced elsewhere and imported for local sales as well as for export to other states, i.e., interstate sales. It has attained the status of a major distribution centre by virtue of its geographical location and other historical factors, availability of infrastructure facilities etc. That it is a major distribution centre borne out by the fact that 49% of fuel oil, 47% of foodgrains, 44% of iron and steel and 78% of fruits and vegetables imported into Delhi are re-exported. The wholesale markets in Delhi deal with about 27 major commodities, covering textiles, auto parts and machinery, stationery, food items and iron and steel etc.

TRADE IN NON-AGRICULTURAL PRODUCTS

The work of the Trade for Development Programme (TDP) on non-agricultural goods focuses on the implications of trade liberalization for developing countries' capacity to develop and sustain a robust industrial base, to diversify their economic structures, to participate in the dynamic sectors of world trade and generate industrial employment. This work also concentrates on the market access conditions met by developing countries exports in international market and the ability of developing countries to use tariffs, subsidies, local content and performance requirements, export taxes and restrictions. Information available under the Value Added Tax (VAT), work force data from population census and gross state domestic products estimates do provide some meaningful estimates on the relative importance of the sector. The income from trade, hotels and restaurant in Delhi constituted ₹ 83539 crore during 2018-19 at current prices, which is nearly 12.44 per cent of Gross

State Domestic Product of Delhi (base year 2011-12). More clearly this sector's contribution to Gross State Domestic Product of Delhi during the last seven years was more than 12 per cent.

SIXTH ECONOMIC CENSUS

As per the Sixth Economic Census there were 8.75 lakhs establishments working in Delhi during 2013, as compared to 7.58 lakhs establishments in 2005 at the time of the fifth Economic Census, registering an annual growth of 1.94%. Also, out of 8.75 lakhs enterprises, only 12,441 (1.4%) were in the rural area and 8.63 lakhs (98.6%) were operated in the urban area. Out of 8.75 lakhs establishments, around 7.96 lakhs (91%) establishments were under private proprietorship, while around 4.70 lakhs (53.7%) worked outside household with fixed structure and remaining 4.05 lakhs (46.3%) were operated outside household without fixed structure of inside household.

ROLE OF THE UN-ORGANISED TRADING SECTOR IN DELHI

Directorate of Economics & Statistics conducted a survey during 1997 on un-organised trading activity in Delhi under the 53rd National Sample Survey Round (State Sample) sponsored by NSSO, Government of India. The coverage of the survey included two types of enterprises, *i.e.*, Own Account Trading Enterprises (OATEs) operated by household members without any hired workers and Non-Directory Trading Enterprises (NDTEs) run with at least one hired worker on fairly regular basis but less than 6 workers including family members. The survey estimated the total number of unorganised trading enterprises as 1.99 lakhs and the number of persons employed as 3.18 lakhs in Delhi. The contribution of this sector which is measured in terms of Gross Value Added to the economy of Delhi was estimated at ₹ 1.01 lakhs per enterprise per annum. No further sample survey has been conducted on this subject after 1997.

ROLE OF THE UN-ORGANISED SERVICE SECTOR IN DELHI

Directorate of Economics and Statistics, Government of NCT of Delhi conducted a survey between July 2006 and June 2007 on un-organized service sector activity in Delhi under the 63rd National Sample Survey Round (State Sample). The total number of enterprises were 239447 and out of these 147281 (61.51 per cent) were Own Account Enterprises (Enterprises operating without any hired worker) and 92166 (38.49 per cent) were Establishment operating with at least one hired worker. The total employment provided by the un-organized service sector was about 6.44 lakh. The gross value Added per annum per enterprises in the un-organized service sector was ₹ 2.87 lakh. The Value Added per worker in this sector was estimated as ₹ 106895 per year. Value added per worker in OAE's was ₹ 70372 and that of establishment was ₹ 119996 per annum.

MARKETING OF AGRICULTURAL PRODUCE

Marketing of agricultural produce in Delhi is through a network of regulated markets. The Delhi Agricultural Marketing Board (DAMB) is the apex body established in 1977 under the Delhi Agricultural Produce Marketing (Regulation) Act., 1976 which was replaced subsequently by a new Act in 1998. The Board exercises supervision and control over various agricultural produce markets and promotes better marketing of agricultural produce by developing infrastructure facilities and providing facilities for grading and standardization.

At present, there are seven principal markets functioning in Delhi.

DELHI AGRICULTURAL MARKETING BOARD (DAMB)

DAMB was established in 1977 under the provisions of Delhi Agricultural Produce Marketing (Regulation) Act, 1976 which has since been replaced by Delhi Agricultural Produce Marketing (Regulation) Act, 1998. The said Act was enacted for the better regulation of the purchase, sale, and storage and processing of agricultural produce and for the establishment of markets of agricultural produce in the National Capital Territory of Delhi and for markets connected therewith or incidental thereto. Under this Act organizational set up has been given to regulate the trading activity of the agricultural produce in the National Capital Territory of Delhi. Delhi Agricultural Marketing Board is an apex body of this organisational set up and its main functions are to provide for general improvements in the markets for their respective areas and to provide facilities for grading and standardisation of agricultural produce.

❒ ❒ ❒

13 Housing

AS the new capital of free India, the city of New Delhi was planned as a garden city, around a central vista with the Secretariat Complex at its western end and the National Stadium at its eastern end. A city centre, known as the Connaught Place Complex, was also established. In order to ameliorate the living conditions of the residents of Delhi and shift the excess population, Delhi Improvement Trust was set up in 1937. Thus, land belonging to the government, known as *Nazul* land, was placed at the disposal of the Trust. As the Delhi Improvement Trust did not succeed in bringing about the desired improvement, especially in the wake of influx of refugees into the capital pursuant to the partition of the country, a Town Planning office was set up in 1955 to prepare a detailed plan for the development of urban Delhi. With the assistance of the Ford Foundation Consultants, the organisation prepared an Interim General Plan. Simultaneously, the government set up a Provisional Development Authority in October, 1955, with the responsibility of preventing bad layout of the land, haphazard execution of buildings or growth of sub-standard colonies and ensuring development and expansion of Delhi according to proper plans.

DELHI DEVELOPMENT AUTHORITY

The Delhi Development Authority (DDA) was established in 1957. Its objective is "to promote and secure the development of Delhi according to Plan." For this purpose, the Authority had the power to acquire, hold, manage and dispose of land and other property, carry out building, engineering, mining and other operations, execute tasks in connection with the supply of water and electricity, disposal of sewage and other services and amenities.

In order to ensure integrated and planned development, the Master Plan of Delhi, which came into force on 1.9.1962, provided the necessary framework for the planned development of Delhi. DDA has, from the very beginning, played a role in every such activity as is connected directly or indirectly with the development of Delhi. The functions of DDA can be broadly categorised as: acquisition and assembly of land for residential, industrial, commercial, institutional and recreational purposes; construction of houses, resettlement of squatters; construction of recreational centres and sports complexes; development infrastructure facilities for smooth functioning of the city like bus terminus, flyovers etc.; construction of commercial district centres, local and convenient shopping centres etc.; relocation of industries from non-conforming areas to conforming areas and development of Industrial Estates; provision of basic services and amenities for such developed areas; development and preservation green of areas and historical monuments.

UNAUTHORIZED COLONIES

During 1993, a list of all unauthorized colonies in Delhi was prepared by Urban Development Department, which indicates that there were 1071 such unauthorized colonies. Due to litigation and other policy issues, no decision could be taken about regularization of such colonies. Government of Delhi started a Plan Scheme in 1997-98 for providing minimum civic services, i.e., construction of road, roadside drain and filling up of low lying area so as to maintain hygienic conditions in these colonies. To meet the expense on provision of water supply, sewerage, roads, drains, sanitation, street lighting and electrification etc, an expenditure of ₹ 6886.92 crore has been incurred till March 2017.

It is estimated that in Delhi there are 1797 Un-authorised Colonies, which are to be regularized as per government policy. These have about 40 lakh population which needs to be effectively incorporated in the mainstream of urban development. This requires provision of infrastructure services and facilities for which differential norms and procedure have been devised.

SLUM FREE CITY

Government of India announced a new scheme called Rajiv Awas Yojana (RAY) under JNNURM for the slum dwellers and the urban poor people envisages a 'Slum-free city' through the active participation of States/ Union Territories to tackle the problem of slums in cities. The main objectives are:

- Bringing existing slums within the formal system and enabling them to avail of the same level of basic amenities as in the rest of the town.

- Redressing the failures of the formal system that lie behind the creation of slums and

- Tackling the shortages of urban land and housing that keep shelter out of reach of the urban poor and force them to resort to extra-legal solutions in a bid to retain their sources of livelihood and employment.

Under this scheme States/Union Territories have to undertake preparatory activities of conducting slum survey, mapping of slums, developing slum information system, undertaking community mobilization, preparation of Slum-free City/State Slum-free Plans before seeking support under Rajiv Awas Yojana. The Government of NCT of Delhi has already submitted a detailed proposal to the Government of India for undertaking slum survey, mapping of slums, developing slum information system, undertaking community mobilization etc. An amount of ₹ 9.78 crore has been received from the Government of India for this project.

JHUGGI JHOPRI CLUSTERS

The inception of slums or jhuggi jhopri clusters started with the development of cities. In Delhi the formation of slums observed even before Independence. The main reasons behind the formation of slum clusters were due to various factors such as flow of migrants from neighbouring states for livelihood and employment. The condition was manageable before 1970 and most of slums were resettled. After 1970, the high pace of development of Delhi and slow development in other states in northern India speeded up the flow of migration to Delhi resulting in massive increase in slum and J.J. Clusters.

The exact number of J.J. Clusters was enumerated in a survey conducted by Government of Delhi in 1990. The survey report mentioned that there were 929 slum clusters and around 2.59 lakh households in Delhi. Delhi Urban Shelter Improvement Board estimated the number of jhuggi jhopri clusters and slum population of Delhi during the year 2010. It is estimated that there are 675 slum clusters with 4 lakh households having a population of 20 lakh in Delhi.

DELHI URBAN SHELTER IMPROVEMENT BOARD (DUSIB)

Delhi Urban Shelter Improvement Board has come into existence under Delhi Urban Shelter Improvement Board Act, 2010, passed by the Legislative Assembly of the National Capital Territory of Delhi on the 1st April, 2010.

DUSIB is primarily responsible for the qualitative improvement of slum settlements and providing various kinds of services for slum dwellers in the city. It also undertakes works relating to provision of shelters to the urban poor/slum dwellers under the policy for relocation of slum and J.J. dwellers, including the provisions of built up flats under exceptional circumstances, when the properties/katras become dangerous/unfit for human habitation. The main thrust is to provide minimal civic infrastructural facilities like toilets, bathrooms and Basti Vikas Kendras (Community Centres) in J.J. Clusters.

TRANS YAMUNA AREA DEVELOPMENT BOARD

For development of Trans Yamuna area in a proper, speedy and sustained manner, Trans Yamuna Area Development Board (TYADB), an advisory Board was constituted in 1994. The Board approves and recommends works for the development of infrastructure in Trans Yamuna area. Various agencies are involved in the development of infrastructure facilities in Trans Yamuna area such as Delhi Jal Board, Municipal Corporation of Delhi, Public Works Department, Department of Irrigation and Flood Control and Urban Development. After the inception of Board, most of the activities relating to the development of infrastructure in Trans Yamuna area are coordinated by the Board.

DEVELOPMENT OF WALLED CITY—DELHI

For maintaining the original heritage character and to improve the environment in the walled city area, a comprehensive redevelopment plan has been prepared. It involves the active participation of governmental and non-governmental agencies and professionals for rejuvenating and maintaining the heritage areas. For ensuring the development of Walled city of Delhi, Delhi Development Authority (DDA) has signed a Memorandum of Understanding (MoU) with the Barcelona Strategic Urban Systems, AIE, Spain during October 2010. The MoU clearly narrated the co-operation in the fields of urban planning, heritage conservation, urban renewal of walled city and its extension etc. Both DDA and Barcelona City Council have decided to undertake joint research activities in Shajahanabad–needs a special treatment to conserve its heritages value while retaining the residential character and listed redevelopment of government owned and private properties in walled city.

❏ ❏ ❏

14 Environmental Concerns

WITH the sustained efforts put in by the Government of Delhi alongwith the cooperation of all stakeholders, Delhi is showing signs of improvement in reducing/controlling the pollution level since past few years.

NOISE POLLUTION

Delhi witnesses excessive noise on account of large number of vehicle of all sorts including those who come from other areas where CNG is not the fuel, construction activities, diesel generating sets, etc. Use of high sound loudspeakers during festivals and many social gatherings in public place directly increases the noise pollution in the affected areas. GNCTD has notified an area of 100 metres around the hospitals with 100 beds or more, educational institutions with 1000 students or more, all court complexes, all government complexes as Silence Areas/Zones. The Central Pollution Control Board published the information regarding permitted ambient noise levels in different areas.

AMBIENT NOISE STANDARDS BY CPCB (IN LEQ/DB(A))

Zones/Areas	Night Time (10 PM to 6 AM)	Day Time (6 AM to 10 PM)
Silence Areas/Zones	40	50
Residential Area	45	55
Commercial Area	55	65
Industrial Area	70	75

WATER POLLUTION

The 48-km stretch of the Yamuna River in Delhi is heavily polluted on account of uncontrolled flow of untreated sewage and also of direct discharge of industrial chemical wastewater. The river water upstream of Wazirabad is fit for drinking after treatment. However, after the confluence of the Najafgarh drain and 24 other major drains which are down stream of Wazirabad barrage, the water quality becomes heavily degraded and is unfit even for animal consumption and irrigation. These 24 major drains pollute Yamuna River for various reasons including due to overflow of untreated sewage from unsewered areas. River Yamuna is monitored for water quality at 9 locations every month and 24 drains are being monitored monthly. DJB has decided to lay interceptor sewers for cleaning Yamuna River. Engineers India Limited has been appointed as Project Management Consultant [PMC] for this project and an escrow account has been created.

DOMESTIC WASTE WATER (SEWAGE) MANAGEMENT

In Delhi, the waste water generated in unplanned area is discharged into drains in the absence of sewerage network. The major cause of concern is non-utilization of installed capacity of sewage Treatment Plants as at present only about 341.39 MGD sewage is being treated by all STPs against their installed capacity of 512.40 MGD. With a view to reduce flow of untreated sewage with Yamuna. 23 sewage treatment plants have already been commissioned. Delhi Jal Board has prepared a plan to provide sewerage facilities in unauthorized colonies which are proposed to be regularized shortly. This will, however, be subject to feasibility. In such areas, about 1000 public toilets have been constructed with JBIC funds, in addition to public toilets being constructed by Slum Wing under their plan scheme. Decentralized system of waste water treatment is the only possible solution to this problem. DJB is contemplating to prepare a feasible plan for this purpose. MCD has also appointed consultant under YMP-II for this purpose.

DJB initiated the process of lying of interceptor sewers along 3 major drains (Najafgarh Drain, Supplementary Drain and Shahadra Drain). Sewage generated from the colonies will be trapped before reaching into major drains and diverted to the existing unutilized STPs/ new STPs. DPR has been prepared.

All major hotels, hospitals, construction projects have been directed to setup STP/ETP for treatment of their wastewater and its effective usages for toilet flushing, cooling tower and horticulture. As a result,

150 such projects have either installed or are in the process of installing such systems which are expected to reduce load on the DJB network substantially. Many hospitals are also setting up such units and recycling the wastewater for horticulture purpose.

YAMUNA ACTION PLAN (PHASE II & III)

Yamuna Action Plan–Phase II (YAP II) is one of the major programme, implemented in Delhi by Delhi Jal Board. It is being implemented in three states of the country (Haryana, Delhi and Uttar Pradesh). During the first phase of the programme, it came out that the river water pollution cannot be lowered down without the active participation of the citizens. Therefore in YAP phase II, a special component named as Public Participation and Awareness has been brought in wherein Non-Governmental Organisations (NGOs) are partnering to work at the community level on different identified themes. These themes include;

- Socio-economic up-gradation of the Community Toilet Complexes neighbourhood as the name suggests, the NGOs involved have to improve the lives and environment of the community residing in the neighbourhood of the community toilets.

- School health and hygiene programme wherein school going children have been targeted to sensitise upon the need for maintaining personal hygiene and sanitation.

- Town Specific innovation programme wherein NGOs are given a flexibility to design and develop a programme specific to the town requirements and could be one of the most innovative approaches and not necessarily duplicating the target groups.

- The entire area of Delhi has been declared as notified area for regulation of ground water. No drawl of ground water without prior permission of DJB and permission shall be granted subject to the condition of installation of rain water harvesting system/treatment of all wastewater and effective reuse of treated water.

E-WASTE MANAGEMENT

Ministry of Environment & Forest (MoEF), GOI has notified E-Waste Management and Handling Rules in May 2011 to come into force from 1st May, 2012. Delhi Govt. has taken several initiatives for creating awareness about E-Waste/E-Waste Rules. E-Waste bins have been provided at various market locations, schools and Govt. offices for collection of e-waste. CPCB has designated authorized recyclers for E-Waste and one collection centre/agency has also been designated by Delhi Govt.

CLIMATE CHANGE MITIGATION MEASURES

On the issue of Combating Climate Change, Delhi is the first city in the country to set a mandate and brought out a detailed Climate Change Agenda for 2009-2012, on the lines of National Action Plan for Climate Change released by the Government of India.

65 important point climate change agenda have been identified for the city of Delhi under following sectors:

(a) Enhanced Energy Efficiency

(b) Sustainable Habitat

(c) Green India

(d) Water Mission

(e) Strategic Knowledge

(f) Solar Mission

SOLAR LIGHTING & HEATING SYSTEM

Energy Efficiency and Renewable Energy Management Centre, Department of Environment, Govt. of Delhi has taken no. of steps to promote solar water heating systems in Delhi such as providing Rebate/ Incentive of ₹ 6000/- for Domestic consumer (Residential accommodation) and up to ₹ 60000 to Non-Commercial institutes depending on capacity of system. Capital Subsidy @ ₹ 3300/- per sq. m. for Flat plate collector and @ ₹ 3000/- per sq. m. for Evacuated tube collectors for domestic as well as commercial and non-commercial establishments is provided through Ministry of New & Renewable Energy. The installation of Solar Water Heater has also been made mandatory in different categories of buildings like Industries, Hotels, Hospitals, Canteens, Corporate and residential building having area of 500 sq. meters or above, Government buildings, etc.

Lightening & illumination through Solar Photovoltaic Power plant of 10.4 kwp at Safdarjung Tomb, New Delhi and 9.0 kwp at Jantar Mantar, New Delhi have been commissioned.

RAIN-WATER HARVESTING STRUCTURE

Installation of Rain-Water Harvesting System has been made mandatory for plots having area of 100 sq. meters and above. The financial assistance of the 50 per cent of the project cost or ₹ 1 lakh whichever is less, is provided by Delhi Government/Delhi Jal Board to the Resident Welfare Associations or Schools for this purpose.

For Hotels/Malls/Construction Projects etc, installation of Rain-Water Harvesting System has been made mandatory through contract mechanism.

❏ ❏ ❏

Geography 15

LOCATION AND AREA

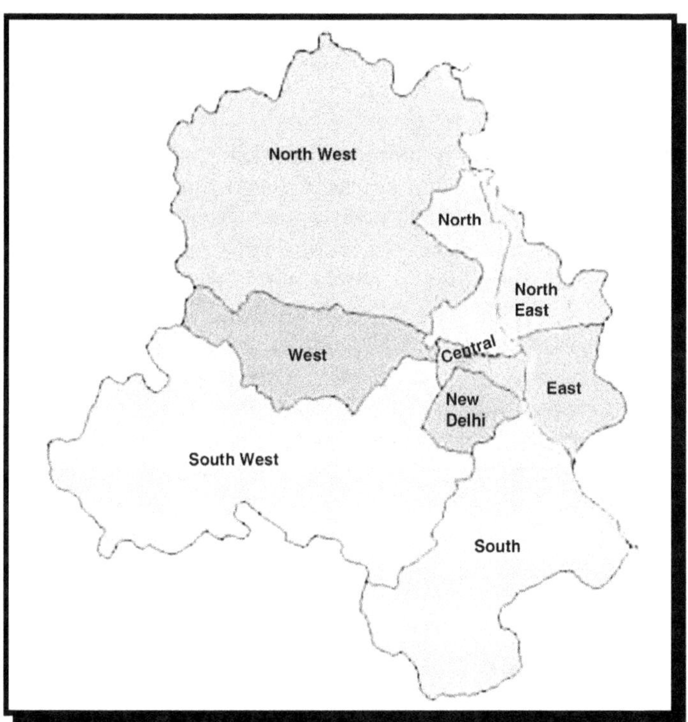

The National Capital Territory of Delhi with an area of 1483 sq. kms. is situated between the Himalayas and Aravallis range in the north-western region of the Indian subcontinent. The major part of its territory lies on the western side of Yamuna. However, a sizeable portion lies on the eastern side of the river. Delhi's altitude ranges between 213 and 305 m above the Mean Sea Level (MSL). It is a narrow strip of

Indo-Gangetic plain lying between 28°25' and 28°53' North Latitude and 76°50' and 77°21' East Longitude. It is surrounded by the state of Haryana on the north, west and south (with borders of districts Sonepat, Rohtak, Gurugram and Faridabad) and by U.P. on the east (with borders of districts Ghaziabad and Noida). The territory of Delhi is divided by river Yamuna, which flows from north to south through the city. Delhi's greatest length and breadth is 51.90 kms. and 48.48 kms., respectively. The general slope of its land is from north to south.

GEOGRAPHICAL FEATURES

In geographical terms, the National Capital Territory of Delhi can be divided into three segments: the Yamuna Flood Plains, the Ridge and the Plains.

KHADAR

The Yamuna flood plains are somewhat low-lying, sandy and are subject to recurrent floods. This area is also called Khadar. During the rainy season, the flood water inundates this region. After these floods subside the moisture in the soil lasts for some time making the land more fertile. The Khadar area has a highly sandy soil. The water table is fairly high, thus facilitating irrigation from wells. The tract lying to the north of the ridge and to the west of Grand Trunk road, which separates it from the Khadar area, is a level plain, known as Bangar. The general level of the Bangar area is higher than that of the Khadar area. The former's water table is comparatively lower. It is characterised by patches of saline efflorescence; these patcher are the result of the composition of the alluvium and a gentle slope of the land. The western Yamuna canal, which traverses the Bangar area, offers satisfactory irrigation facility to this tract.

THE RIDGE

The ridge constitutes the most dominating physiographic feature of this territory. It originates from the Aravali hills of Rajasthan, entering the Union Territory of Delhi from the south and extending towards a north-easternly direction. It encircles the city on its north-west and west. A branch of the ridge separates itself from the main trunk near Bhatti and extends towards north-easternly direction up to Arangpur. At Arangpur, it turns north-west till it rejoins the main ridge in the shape of a sweeping curve. The point near Bhatti has a height of 1045 ft. Tughlakabad Fort is located on one of the highest spurs of the ridge.

The whole space between the river Yamuna and the ridge has a triangular shape with an apex at Wazirabad and the base extending between Tughlakabad and Mehrauli. This shape has been the site of various cities. The southern portion of land near Mehrauli and Tughlakabad is known as Kohi (hilly). Due to inadequacy of water and rocky nature of the terrain, the ridge is generally devoid of vegetation. At best, it supports some stunted trees of Kikar and Karil, thorny shrubs, bushes of Ber and other similar varieties. There are traces of thin laminae of mica over its surface, which shines brightly under the tropical Sun. The water table is low and traditional irrigation is impracticable. Quarrying has been done on a fairly large scale and there are a number of disused quarries, which have become reservoirs of water. These water bodies attract animals and birds.

DABAR

The Dabar is the low basin situated towards the west of the hills. It includes Najafgarh and Kakrola areas, which are adjacent to Palam village. There is a depression near the Najafgarh township where water from the western side of the ridge accumulates during the rainy season. The drainage of the hills accumulates in this natural receptacle. In the year of good rains, an area of 51.8 sq kms. or so gets flooded. Even during the winter months, the depression occupies an area of about 12 sq kms. Had the Najafgarh escape channel not carried away a part of the waters to the Yamuna, a much larger area of depression region would have been inundated.

THE PLAINS

Leaving aside the Yamuna flood plain (Khadar) and the ridge, the entire area of the National Capital Territory of Delhi is categorised as Bangar or the Plain. A major portion of the area of Delhi is plain and on this are located Delhi, New Delhi and Delhi Cantonment along with a vast stretch of numerous villages. The land of the plain is mostly fertile.

RIVERS AND CANALS

Yamuna is the main river, which passes through the territory. Apart from the flood channels of Yamuna, there are three canals viz. portion of Agra canal, Hindon canal and western Yamuna canal.

In Delhi, the general slope of the land is from north to south. A local watershed, which visible on the western side of the river, divides the drainage system of that region into two sectors. While the eastern part drains itself into the Yamuna, the surface water of the western region passes through natural depressions southwards into the Najafgarh drain.

YAMUNA

The Yamuna, one of the ancient water courses of northern India, forms the chief drainage channel of the territory. The river has been flowing through the land of Delhi for millennia and has left rich deposits of alluvium on its either bank. The river enters the union territory from the north of Palla village, at an altitude of nearly 690 ft. above sea level and leaves it near Jaitpur near Okhla at an altitude of 650 ft. above MSL. Its course within the limits of Delhi extends roughly over form the 51 kms. During the rainy season, the river extends considerably in breadth, swelling at some places to several kms. The maximum depth in this season is about 25 ft. and its discharge at Okhla is above 4100 cusecs. In the dry weather, however, the river becomes shallow and narrow its maximum depth dwindles to about 4 ft. and the discharge to less than 200 cusecs. Having been drained of its waters to a considerable extent by the two canals before it enters the territory, the Yamuna meanders across the plains of Delhi as a stream, almost at every point, except during the rains. The river is flanked by low sandy banks on its either side, though a firm rock has also been detected in the bed at the Okhla weir. The banks of the river are strengthened by bends and embankments to check floods.

FLOODS

The Yamuna has a long history of heavy floods, which are mainly caused by the heavy rainfall in the catchment areas of the remote mountainous regions. The tendency to get the deluge is aided by the inadequate capacity of the river to carry the full flood discharge and the flat nature of the land. When in spate, the river encroaches upon the cultivated Khadar lands on its both sides. Adjacent villages get marooned and much havoc to life and property is caused. The floods are generally confined on the left bank, to the rural areas between the river and the right bank of the eastern Yamuna canal, and also, between the river and the Delhi-Karnal Grand Trunk road on the right bank. A number of severe floods have been recorded during the recent past in the years 1924, 1955, 1958, 1964, 1967 and 1978.

LAKES

The Najafgarh lake, lying along the Delhi-Haryana border to the extreme south, is the largest natural depression. This saucer-shaped lake is situated near the Najafgarh village, at a distant of about 32.2 kms. due south-west of the main city. During rainy seasons, the lake is filled by water from its own catchment. Another depression is located to the north of Bhalaswa Jahangirpuri along the Grand Trunk road in its Delhi-Karnal stretch. It is a horseshoe lake and probably a remnant of the old Yamuna, when it followed a more westerly course.

UNDERGROUND WATER

The ground water resources of Delhi are limited and their utilization for irrigation on a large scale is not possible. Further, extensive chemical tests have revealed that except for a few isolated wells, underground water of the region is generally brackish and unfit for drinking or irrigation.

SEISMIC PHENOMENA

Delhi lies in a belt that is prone to earthquakes of moderate intensity. Slight tremors not felt by people are recorded by seismographs several times in a year. During recent years, the epicentres of many earthquakes of low intensities have been recorded within 100 kms. These earthquakes are due to faults—the Sohna fault and the Hidden Moradabad fault. Besides the earthquakes from these sources, the region is also affected by large ones occurring in the highly seismic Himalayan region and Kutch. Out of the ten important earthquakes felt in Delhi during the past few centuries, five had their origins near Delhi. These were recorded in 1720, 1956, 1962 and 1964. The maximum damage was caused by the earthquake of 1803; in this catasteophe, the top storey of the Qutub Minar was destroyed.

TOWNS, VILLAGES AND AMENITIES

Prior to the shift of the capital from Calcutta (now Kolkata), Delhi comprised the tehsils of Delhi, Sonepat and Ballabgarh, with a total area of 1276 square miles. In 1912, a separate Delhi province was formed; it comprised the Delhi tehsil and a small portion of the Ballabhgarh tehsil. In 1915, an area of 46 sq. miles on the eastern banks of the Yamuna was transferred to Delhi from the Ghaziabad tehsil of the United Provinces. Thereafter, Delhi has not undergone any change in its geographical limits except for a few marginal modifications.

The administrative boundaries of NDMC and Delhi Cantonment remained unchanged during the decade 1991-2001 but the area of Delhi Municipal Corporation (Urban) underwent a change due to urbanisation of certain villages. The total area of Delhi Municipal Corporation (Urban) which was 360.55 sq. kms. at the time of 1981 Census, rose to 925 sq. kms. in 2001 due to urbanisation of these villages. The urban population is distributed among 113 towns, out of which, 3 towns, New Delhi Municipal Council (NDMC), Delhi Cantonment (Delhi Cantonment) and Delhi Municipal Corporation (Urban) (DMC-U) are statutory towns and the remaining 110 are Census Towns (CTs). There are 112 villages in Delhi. The rural area is 369.35 sq. kms while the urban area is spread over 1113.65 sq. kms.

WEATHER AND CLIMATE

Delhi has an extreme climate, which is very cold in winter and terribly hot in summer. The cold season begins in November and is at its peak around the time of the New Year and the first half of January. After the middle of March, the weather tends to be warm and soon, it becomes hot. In April, the weather becomes hot with no movement of air. In May and June, the temperatures climb to 45 degrees Celsius. The monsoons arrive in Delhi towards the end of June. These could arrive early in some years and could also be late by some days. The monsoon rains last till September. During this period, the weather can become extremely humid. Delhi does not have much rainfall but there are nearly 50 wet days in the year in which, there is some significant rainfall. Like most of the areas of northern India, Delhi has a rainy season in winter also and invariably, there is rainfall in December and January and sometimes in, February also. For the farmers of the villages in the National Capital Territory, the winter rain is important because the Rabi crop gets benefit by it.

The weather in Delhi touches extreme hot and cold during different parts of the year. The winter or the cold season starts towards the latter half of November when both day and night temperatures drop rapidly. January is the coldest month with the mean daily maximum temperature of 21.3°C and the mean daily minimum temperature of 7.3°C. From the middle of March, temperatures begin to rise fairly rapidly. May and June are the hottest months. While day temperatures are higher in May, the nights are warmer in June. From April onwards, the hot wind starts blowing and makes the weather unpleasant. In May and June maximum temperatures may sometimes reach 46° or 47°C. With the advance of the monsoon into the area towards the end of June or the beginning of July, day temperatures drop appreciably while the night temperatures remain high. In October, the day temperatures are almost the same as the ones in the monsoon months but the nights are cooler. Delhi is most comfortable between October and February, with daytime temperatures of around 71.5 degree F (22 degrees C) and cool evenings. December and January are decidedly chilly, with night-time lows of upto 39 degrees F (4 degrees C). The city has a fleeting but beautiful flowering splendour during the spring months of February and March, when parks brim with flowers. The summer months of May and June are scorching, with the mercury soaring to a high of 115 degrees F (46 degrees C).

In Delhi, the climate is mainly influenced by its inland position and the prevalence of air of the continental type during the major part of the year. Extreme dryness, along with an intensely hot summer and cold winter, is the characteristic of the climate. Only during the three monsoon months—July, August and September—does air of oceanic origin penetrate this region and causes increased humidity, cloud cover and precipitation. The year can be divided into four seasons. The cold season starts in late November and extends up to the beginning of March. This is followed by the hot season, which lasts till the end of June, when the monsoon arrives over the territory. The monsoon continues till the last week of September. The two post-monsoon months—October and November—constitute transition periods from the monsoon to winter conditions. The month of September wintnesses the retreat of monsoon winds.

RAINFALL

The average annual rainfall over Delhi is 714 mm. The rainfall in the territory increases from the south-west to the north-east. About 80 per cent of the annual rainfall is received during monsoon months of July, August and September. The rest of the annual rainfall is received as winter rains and as thunderstorm rains in the pre-monsoon and post-monsoon months.

HUMIDITY

The air over Delhi is dry during the greater part of the year. Humidity is high in the monsoon months. April and May are the driest months with relative humidity of about 30 per cent in the mornings and less than 20 per cent in the afternoons.

WINDS

Winds are generally light in the post-monsoon and winter months. These strengthen in the summer and monsoon months. Except during the monsoon months, winds are predominantly from westerly or north-westerly direction and tend to be more northerly in the afternoons. Easterly and south-easterly winds are more common in the monsoon months. April to June is the period with the highest incidence of thunderstorms and dust storms. Some thunderstorms give rise to violent squalls *(andhis)*. While some of the thunderstorms are dry, others are accompanied by heavy rains and less frequently, with hailstorms. Thunderstorms also occur in the winter months in conjunction with western disturbances. Fog, sometimes dense, occurs in the extreme winter months.

▌ NATURAL WEALTH ▌

MINERALS

Delhi does not have minerals of economic importance except some building and materials comprising sand, stone and *(bajri)*. The quartzite rock available on the ridge is very useful for the manufacture of stoneware and buildings. Kaolin is used as a principal raw material for refractory industries, fire clay, for brick manufacture and chinaware. The Delhi quartzite rocks available on the ridge provide inexhaustible supplies of building and road-making materials. The stone quarries in the ridge area have been shut down since 1984 on account of environmental considerations.

THE FLORA

The geographical location, sub-tropical climate and physiographic features affect Delhi's vegetation cover. The natural vegetation of this region is a synthesis of the arid regions of Rajasthan, drier regions of the Upper Gangetic Plain and plains of Haryana. According to the climate, there are three distinct vegetation seasons. The overall climate is, however, unfavourable for the growth of any luxuriant vegetation. Most of the plants found on the ridge, in valleys, on flat slopes, in trenches and ponds and along river banks, are naturally occurring. Some others, though not indigenous, have become naturalized. Trees are sparse, of medium sizes and thorny. Nonetheless, owing to the low rainfall and the gravelly substratum, the upper stratum of the soil does not support any dense perennial vegetation. Thus, during part of the year the climate and soil conditions of Delhi favour a semi-desert vegetation. The flora of Delhi comprises nearly 1000 species of flowering plants, belonging to nearly 120 families. Nearly 60 per cent of the species are indigenous or naturalised and the remaining ones are either introduced or cultivated. The flora of Delhi is a blend of natural vegetation (represented by the plants of the ridge area and on the banks of the Yamuna) and the cultivated plants (represented by gardens, parks and avenues). More than 50 per cent of the indigenous flora comprises tropical and cosmopolitan species. Out of the exotics, nearly 8 per cent are from tropical Africa, less than 5 per cent from the New World and nearly 2 per cent from the temperate areas. There are no endemic in this region.

THE FORESTS

The forest cover has increased from 0.76% of total area in 1980-81 to 1.75% in 1994-95 and 12.97% in 2017. A spur of the Aravalli hills of Rajasthan, spread across the territory of Delhi in the south-west-north-east direction, is called Delhi Ridge. The ridge and its neighbouring hilly tracts represent the natural flora, which is a tropical, thorny and secondary forest. The greater of the reserved forest of this territory is located on the New Delhi ridge, opposite to the Rashtrapati Bhavan at the back of Laxmi Narain Temple. The vegetation of the ridge can be grouped into two broad categories, which are: (i) permanent vegetation and (ii) ephemeral vegetation.

DISTRICT-WISE FOREST COVER IN DELHI (sq. Km)

Districts	Geo-graphical Area	Very Dense Forest	Mod. Dense Forest	Open Forest	Total	% of GA
Central Delhi	25	0.00	2.08	2.86	4.94	19.76
East Delhi	64	0.00	1.05	2.65	3.7	5.78

Districts	Geo- graphical Area	Very Dense Forest	Mod. Dense Forest	Open Forest	Total	% of GA
New Delhi	35	1.69	5.47	9.25	16.41	46.89
North Delhi	59	0.00	2.83	1.75	4.58	7.76
North-East Delhi	60	0.00	0.99	2.99	3.98	6.63
North-West Delhi	440	0.09	8.72	8.74	17.55	3.99
South Delhi	250	2.59	17.68	63.08	83.35	32.34
South-West Delhi	421	2.35	14.86	33.89	51.1	12.14
West Delhi	129	0.00	2.56	4.24	6.8	5.27
Grand Total	**1,483**	**6.72**	**56.24**	**129.45**	**192.41**	**12.97**

ASOLA BHATTI WILD LIFE SANCTUARY

Asola Bhatti Wildlife Sanctuary spread over 6,800 acres is situated near Tughlakabad Fort in South Delhi. The Wildlife Sanctuary is considered the breathing lung of the cosmopolitan city of Delhi. It was established in 1992 with the aim to protect the wildlife in the area between Delhi and Surajkund (Delhi-Haryana border). The Asola Bhatti wildlife sanctuary actually lies in South Delhi District, all along Delhi Haryana Border along Faridabad and Gurugram.

The sanctuary is located on the Southern Ridge which is part of the northern terminal of Aravalli Hills (Aravallis are one of the oldest mountain system of the world). The reason for the biodiversity significance of the Ridge lies in its merger with Indo-Gangetic Plains. The legal Status of the Southern Ridge was considered uncertain till 1986 when the community land of villages Asola, Shapur and Maidangari (4707 Acre) were notified and land of Bhatti mines area (2167 Acre) was notified in 1991 as Sanctuary. About 23 Check dams have been constructed at Asola Wild Life Sanctuary for storing rain water. These check dams have proved to be very effective for ground water recharge and creation of water bodies for the sustenance of Wild Life in the Sanctuary.

DEVELOPMENT AND MANAGEMENT OF RIDGE AREA

The Delhi Ridge, an extension of the Aravali Mountains acts as the green lungs of the city. About 7784 hectares of the Ridge area have been notified as a reserve forest. The Ridge is divided into five portions. The details regarding the management of Delhi Ridge and area in each portion is presented below:

MANAGEMENT OF DELHI RIDGE

Sl. No.	Ridges	Managing Agency	(Area in Ha)
1.	Northern Ridge	Delhi Development Authority, Unified Municipal Corporation of Delhi & Forest Department	87
2.	Central Ridge	Forest Department, Delhi Development Authority, Army, Unified Municipal Corporation of Delhi, Central Public Works Department, New Delhi Municipal Council.	864
3.	South Central Ridge (Near Mehrauli)	Delhi Development Authority	626
4.	Nanakpura South Central	Delhi Development Authority	7
5.	Southern Ridge	Forest Department, Delhi Development Authority, Sports Authority of India	6200
	Total		7784

DEVELOPMENT OF CITY FOREST IN DELHI

Delhi has twelve old city forests. Five city forests are in North-East district, two each in East district and South West and one each in South, North and North West districts respectively. The information regarding the old city forest in Delhi is presented below:

Old City Forests in Delhi–Area and Districts

Sl. No.	Name of City Forest	Area (Hectare)	District
1.	Nasirpur City Forest	28.00	South-West
2.	Alipur City Forest	16.80	North
3.	Hauzrani City Forest	28.80	South
4.	Mitraon City Forest	40.00	South-West
5.	Sultanpur City Forest	48.00	North-West
6.	Ghoga City Forest	10.40	East
7.	Shahapur Garhi City Forest	8.00	North-East
8.	Mamurpur City Forest	56.00	North-East

Sl. No.	Name of City Forest	Area (Hectare)	District
9.	Jindpur City Forest	47.60	North-East
10.	Mukhmelpur City Forest	53.00	North-East
11.	Bawana City Forest	32.00	North-East
12.	Garhi Mandu City Forest	300.00	East

In addition to these 12 old city forests, there are 30 more city forest created during 2007-08 to 2011-12 in Delhi with an area of 795.06 hectare. Thus total area under 42 (12 old and 30 new created) city forests in Delhi is about 1463.66 hectare.

GARDENS

Delhi has been noted for parks and gardens since ancient times. The Mughal Garden rosary is considered to be the finest in Asia. The terraced garden with a central oval pond, the 'showers' of the vermilion-coloured blooms of *Pyrostegia Venusta,* the unending variety of flowering herbs and shrubs, the well-pruned bushes of *Narangi,* laden with golden-brown rotund fruits, the redstone paths and the many fountains make the Mughal Gardens one of the most fascinating natural floral habitats of the globe. Significantly, most of the gardens, which were developed before India's independence, are associated with historical monuments and were created by the rulers of Delhi over centuries. These include the Lodi Garden, Qudsia Garden, Nicholson Park, Roshanara Bagh, and Qutub Garden. These gardens generally present sombre layouts with an abundance of evergreen plants. In addition, Asparagus, Crotons, Jasmines, Rangoon Creeper and other eye-catching creepers, Henna or *Mehndi,* the maroon-coloured bougainvillea and the stately *Roystonea Regia* (bottle palm) are found in plenty.

NEW GARDENS

The gardens, which have been developed after independence, include the Buddha Jayanti Park and Nehru Park. They present an array of foliage and flower plants and also, an admixture of tropical and sub-temperate plants. Developed on the ridge in the Japanese style, the Buddha Jayanti Park has preserved the natural environment of the

Ridge and has, at the same time, added miles of green lawns and colourful shrubbery to it. The park surrounding the Rajghat presents a simple yet serene atmosphere. The trees and shrubs of Rajghat are of both Indian and foreign origins. They include pines, a few other conifers, mangniclias, cassias, banyan, eucalyptus, terminalias, alstonia, pongarnia, thespesia, shisham and many more.

THE AVENUE TREES

The monotony of the roads and buildings of New Delhi is broken by the avenues, which are lined with several flowering trees. These provide soothing shade in the dry summer and when these are in bloom (usually in March - April) these make pleasing sights. *Neem* is the most common of the avenue trees. Among other common avenue trees are the profusely flowering *Amaltas* which, when in bloom, appear like a green canopy bedecked with several chandeliers of yellow bloom, *Aaulsari* whose ripening fruits remain covered by the dense green foliage, Mango, Gulmohur, wild cotton tree, Shisham, Silver Oak, *Kachnar*, *Pipul*, Willow, Eucalyptus, Polvatthia, Jacaranda, Kigelia Dinnata (Candelbra tree) and Lagerstroemia (known as the pride of India) adorn some of the avenues.

FAUNA

Geographically, Delhi falls under the Cis-Gangetic Zoological area. The fauna of the region is characteristically oriental and is fairly rich and varied. It represents various phyla, which range from protozoa to mammals.

ANIMALS

The principal indigenous mammals of Delhi are *Lakarbaggha* (Hayden hyaena) Wolf (Canis lupus) fox (Vulpes begalensis), Jackal (Canis indicus and Canis aureus) and Leopard (Panthera pardus). Leopards, once abundant in the jungles and low forests, are now rarely found in the ravines of the kohi tract, where they prey on the cattle. The Hyaen lives in jungles. It is known to raid hen coops and carry away fowls at night. The common fox, wolf and jackal are nocturnal and predatory in habits. Wolves are fairly common in Khadar and Kohi regions. Foxes and jackals are abundant on lonely hilly ridges. The hedgehog (Hemiechinus) and shrew (Suncus) both belong to an order of mammals called *insectivora*. Hedgehogs, which are found in gardens and shrubs, frequent gardens and houses in cold weather. The common monkey

(Macaca radiata) is the only indigenous primate found in large numbers in suburban orchards and near railway stations.

HOOFED ANIMALS

The Ungulata (hoofed animals) are represented by three genera of antelopes and also, by the wild pig or boar. Wild pigs (Sus cristatus) are found in the Khadar tract. Black bucks (Antilope cervicapra) are found at numerous locations, usually in small herds, each one of these comprising 5-8 animals. However, in the Najafgarh tract and in the vicinity of Mehrauli, the herds are large in numbers. The Indian gazelles are, found in quite small herds. Another member is the large Indian antelope or *Neelgai* (Boselaphus tragocamelus), which exists in very small numbers and its occurrence is seldom reported.

RODENTS

Porcupines, hares, rats and squirrels constitute the rodent fauna of Delhi. The porcupine (Hystrix indica) is very much common. The hare (Lepus nigricollis) is found in abundance in jungles and wooded tracts. Common house rat (Rattus rattus) nocturnal in habit and mouse (Mus dubious) are prolific breeders with a high percentage of population. The white bellied house rats (Rattus rattus rufescence) and brown coloured house rats (Rattus rattus rattus) are also available but these are rather scarce in numbers. The ubiquitous squirrels (Funambulus palmarum) small-sized arboreal rodents, which are found in abundence occurrence.

REPTILES

The crocodile (Crocodilus palustris) is available in the river Yamuna. The commonly found lizards are—house lizard (Hemidactyus flaviviridis), garden lizard (Calotes versicolor) *Brahmini* (Maubuyaa disimillis), sanda (*Vromastix hardwickii*) and gon (*Varanus monitor*). Out of the poisonous snakes, the cobra (Najatripudians) is the most common. Other poisonous snakes are the krait (Bungarus coeruleus) and viper (Viper sp.). The harmless snakes include Topodonotus piccator (found in the lakes and ponds), *dhamin* (zamenis mucusus), rat snake (Zamenis fesciolatus), python (*Python molurus*), worm snake (Typhlops braminus), wolf snake (*Lucodon aulicus*), and dumti (Ervx johnii). The pond turtle (Lissemys punctata) and box turtle (Tronyx genteticus) abound both in the river and lakes.

AMPHIBIANS

Among the amphibians, the toad (Bufo melanosticus) and Indian bull frog (Rana tigrina) are very common.

BIRDS

There are several kinds of birds in Delhi, the most common of these being the house sparrow (Passer domesticus). Yellow throated sparrow is, however, not uncommon in suburbs. Common house-crow (Corvus splendens) provides a common sight everywhere but in unpopulated areas, the jungle crow (Corvus macro- rhynchos), which is jet black in colour, is commonly seen. Crow-pheasant (Cantropus sinensis) is also found in orchards. However, it is rarely seen in populated areas. The wild dove (Streptopelia senegalensis) and jungle babbler (Turdoides striatus) are abundantly found throughout Delhi. Nests of the common weaver-bird (Ploceus philippinus) are found outside the populated areas. Among sea-rangers, the Pariah kite (Milvus migrans) is commonly seen circling high in the sky throughout the year. The Brahmini kite (Haliastur indus), white-backed or Bengal vulture (Gyps bengalensis) are found in large numbers. The resident game birds are mostly grey-patridges (Francolinus francolinus), blue rock pigeons (Columba livia) and common sand grouses, (Pterocles exutus) prefer the sandy tracts of soil. Green pigeons (Crocopus phoenicopterus) and Bush quails (Perdicula asiatica) are found throughout the year. But grey quails or baters (Coturnix) being migratory birds, can be seen in plenty only in the cold weather.

Ducks, snipes and teals (Nettapus coromandelianus) are found in winter wherever ponds and lakes are located. Geese of both forms, the bar headed *Hans* (Anser indicus) and grey-legged *Raj Hans* (Anser anser) are seen along the river Yamuna and around Najafgarh in winter, especially when the gram crop is almost ripe.

Other birds include barnets of several kinds, sunbirds, the Indian roller-*nilkanth* (Coracias benghalensis), several kinds of king fisher (Alcedo atthis), grey hornbill (Tockus birostris) nightjar (Caprimulgus asiaticus), hawk, cuckoo, *koel*, parakeet, owls and owlets of several descriptions as well as eagles, vultures, falcons, harriers, kites, shrikes, tree pies, *mainas*, starlings, tailor-birds, crows, doves, weaver birds, bee eaters, fly catchers, blue throats, robins, swallows, swifts, martins, babblers, *bulbuls*, hoopoe and several kinds of chats, larks and wagtails.

WATER BIRDS

Among water birds, saras, other herons, coots, the Indian darter, snake birds, bitterns, cormorants, sand pipers, plovers, terns, spoonbills, adjutants and several varieties of storks and egrets are included.

FISHES

In Delhi, the fishes are found in the river Yamuna, tanks and ponds. These comprise sixty-five species. The fish fauna can be distinguished into Edible Fish, Ornamental Fish and miscellaneous. Most available fishes in the markets for human consumption are *Singhara* (Mystus seenghala), Mulli (Wallago attu), Rohu (Labeo rohita), Catle (Catla catla), *Kalbons* (Labeo calbasu) *Narain* or *Mrigal* (Cirrhina mrigala, Cirrhina reba), *Mahasher or Raja* (Barbur for), Silond (Silonia silundia), Shouli (Ophiocephalus striatus), Bacha (Eturopichthes vacha), Rita (Rita rita) Balm (Rynchobdella aculeata and Mestacembatus armatus) etc. Ornamental Fishes are also eaten but can serve as good looking aquaria fish. These are *Gaurami* (Colisa fasiata), *Billi* (Botia lohachata), Glass fish (Ambasis ranga), Punti (Puntius sp.), Chela (Chela bachila), young ones of Balms (Rynchobdella aculeata, Mestacembalus armatus), (Esomus dendricus), etc. Other fishes are Labeo gonius, Puntius sarana, Puntius sophore, Crossocheilus latius pungabensis, Amblypharyngodon mola, Mystus aor, Clupisoma garna etc.

INSECTS

The arachnids, comprising julmandal (Galeodes sp.) and scorpions (Buthus, Palamnaeus) are fairly abundant. The isopods (Onisous), centipedes (Scolopendra), millipedes (Thuropygus) and spiders (Epeira) are also very common in Delhi. The insects commonly found are crickets (Gryllus, Gryllodes and Gryllotalpat), cockroaches (Periplanet Blatta), blister beetles (Melve Mylabris), lady bird beetles (Cocindella, Chilomones), beetles (Chcindella, scarabeus), the earwig (Labidura), bugs (Lethocerus, Bagrads and Chysocharis), dragon flies (Pantala, Crocothemis), white ants (Odontoterms, Coptoterms), flies (Musca tabanus, Calliphora), mosquitoes (Ades, Anopheles and culex), the saw fly (Athlia), wasps (Vespa and Polistes), the ants (Comporaotus and solenopsis), the aphids (Aphis and Rhopalosiphum), the butterflies (Papilio, Dansis and Pleris), the moths (Daphnis, Aeries and Acherontia) and the ant-lion (Myrmeles and Culex) etc.

❐ ❐ ❐

Agriculture & Rural Development   16

RAPID urbanization and the growth of trade and industry have significantly reduced the contribution of agriculture sector in Delhi's economy. The share of agriculture and allied activities in the Gross State Domestic Product at current prices in Delhi has declined sharply from 1.40% in 1999-2000 to 0.49% in 2017-18.

LAND HOLDING PATTERN

As economy is moving alongwith rapid urbanization, the agriculture holdings in Delhi is also reducing at a speedy rate. This is evident as per the Agricultural Census. The information regarding the agricultural land holding pattern and area operated for agricultural purposes in Delhi, during the last two agricultural census is presented below:

LAND HOLDINGS & OPERATIONAL AREA IN DELHI: 2010-11 AND 2015-16

Sl. No.	Details	Agricultural Census 2010-11	Agricultural Census 2015-16
1.	**Operational Holdings (Number)**		
	(a) Individual	8195 (39.98)	7960 (38.50)
	(b) Joint	11358 (55.41)	11575 (55.99)
	(c) Institutional	944 (4.61)	1140 (5.51)
	Total	**20497 (100.00)**	**20675 (100.00)**
2.	**Operational Area (in Hectares)**		
	(a) Individual	7087.95 (23.92)	6886.76 (23.79)
	(b) Joint	21341.82 (72.03)	20063.22 (69.31)
	(c) Institutional	1198.44 (4.05)	1995.94 (6.90)
	Total	**29628.21 (100.00)**	**28945.92 (100.00)**

Sources: Agricultural Census 2010-11 & 2015-16

During the last agricultural census conducted during 2005-06, near about three-fifth of the operational holdings size was less than one hectare, commonly called marginal size. Near about one-fifth of the holdings were under the category of small size and the size was in between one and two hectares. Very less percentage of operational holdings was under the category of large holdings and the size was above ten hectares. Area operated in agriculture in Delhi was highest in medium size and it constitutes near about one-third of the total areas operated.

LAND USE PATTERN IN DELHI

As per village records, the total cropped area during 2000-01 was at 52816 hectares, reduced to 36041 hectares in 2005-06 and in 2017-18 was to tune of 34,750 hectares. The reduction of cropped area during this period was worked out at 1.91 per cent per annum. Simultaneously the percentage of cropped area from total area was reduced from 35.81 per cent in 2000-01 to 23.85 per cent in 2015-16. The remaining areas of the Delhi are being used for various other uses such as non-agricultural purposes, forest, fallow land, uncultivable land, etc. The main reasons behind such reduction in agriculture area in Delhi are due to the fast urbanization, and shift in occupational pattern especially during the last two decades. This results in reduction of share of this sector to the Gross State Domestic Product of Delhi.

CROP INTENSITY

Crop intensity is an index of agriculture development and is directly related to irrigation facilities. It is the percentage ratio of gross cropped area to net area sown. It may be measured by the formula-gross cropped area/net sown area x 100. The intensity of cropping, therefore, refers to raising a number of crops from the same field during one agricultural year. The index of cropping intensity is 100 if one crop has been grown in a year and it is 200 if two crops are raised. Higher the index, greater is the efficiency of land use. The cropping intensity has direct correlation with assured irrigation which enables farmers to go for multiple cropping and use higher dose of fertilizers and HYV seeds. Hence, besides irrigation fertilisers, early maturing high yielding variety of seeds, selective mechanization such as the use of tractors, pumping sets and seed drills, etc., plant, protection measures through the use of insecticides, pesticides etc. do have role in affecting the intensity of cropping.

CROP INTENSITY OF DELHI DURING 2000-01 TO 2018-19

Sl. No.	Year	Net Area Sown	Gross Cropped Area	Cropping Intensity (%)
1.	2000-01	34,034	52,816	155
2.	2005-06	23,809	36,957	166
3.	2010-11	22,124	31,366	152
4.	2011-12	22,885	36,445	159
5.	2012-13	23,118	35,178	152
6.	2013-14	23,150	34,312	148
7.	2014-15	23,150	34,312	148
8.	2015-16	23,150	34,312	148
9.	2016-17	23,150	34,750	150
10.	2017-18	23,050	34,700	150
11.	2018-19 (Estd)	22,300	33,455	150

IRRIGATION IN DELHI

Irrigation in Delhi mainly depends upon ground water and partly upon surface water. Irrigation from the ground water is provided through shallow cavity and the deep cavity state tube-wells, whereas surface irrigation provided by way of utilizing treated effluent available from existing sewage treatment plants located at Coronation Pillar, Okhla and Keshopur. Water from Western Yamuna Canal System under the control of Haryana Government is also utilized for irrigation purpose.

SOURCE-WISE IRRIGATED AREA IN DELHI

Sl. No.	Sources	2016-17	2017-18
1.	Canals	2240	2246
2.	Wells	19727	19777
3.	Area Irrigated	21967	22023
4.	Area Irrigated under more than one crop	7756	7775
5.	Gross area Irrigated	29723	29798

ANIMAL HUSBANDRY

Animal Husbandry is the occupation which takes care of domestic animals that are used primarily as food or product sources. It is an important component in the agriculture sector and directly and indirectly affects the development of economy.

The word "livestock" is an umbrella term used for domesticated animals raised in an agricultural environment, with the intent of providing food, textiles, labour, or fertilizer to their owners. Common examples of livestock are horses, pigs, goats, buffaloes, cows, sheep, and poultry, etc. Raising livestock is an important part of life for people all over the world.

LIVESTOCK IN DELHI

Sl. No.	Livestock	Livestock Census (Number)	
		2007	*2012*
1.	Cow	107730	86433
2.	Buffaloes	266626	162142
3.	Sheep	5896	932
4.	Goats	21176	30470
5.	Others	21891	86,420
	Total	**423319**	**360397**

VETERINARY FACILITIES

In Delhi there are 49 Veterinary Hospitals (inc. Vety. Poly. Clinic), 26 Veterinary Dispensaries and 250 private clinics. In addition to these, there are two laboratories/research centre for veterinary facilities in Delhi. The number of veterinary hospitals and veterinary dispensaries in Delhi during the last one decade was more or less the same. That means there is no expansion of veterinary facilities in Delhi.

RURAL DEVELOPMENT

As per 2011 census, total rural area of Delhi was at 369.35 sq. km, i.e., 24.91 per cent of the total area of Delhi and 2.50 per cent of the total population. The number of villages in Delhi reduced from 304 in 1951 to 112 in 2011. The information regarding the villages, rural population during the last seven decade is presented below:

RURAL POPULATION OF DELHI: 1951-2011

Sl. No.	Years	Villages (Number)	Population		
			Rural	Total	% of Rural to Total
1.	1951	304	306938	1744072	17.60
2.	1961	276	299204	2658612	11.25
3.	1971	243	418675	4065698	10.30
4.	1981	214	452206	6220406	7.27
5.	1991	199	949019	9420644	10.07
6.	2001	165	944727	13850507	6.82
7.	2011	112	419042	16787941	2.50

DELHI RURAL DEVELOPMENT BOARD (DRDB)

Delhi Rural Development Board was re-constituted in 2004 with the aim to formulate a unified area plan for rural areas of Delhi and to monitor projects and schemes being implemented by all agencies such as Municipal Corporation of Delhi, Irrigation and Flood Control Department, Development Deptt. The Board's function is to advise the Government on issues connected with the infrastructure development for securing Planned growth of Rural Areas of Delhi.

❒ ❒ ❒

17   Delhi Life Style

DELHI shares its borders with Haryana, Rajasthan, Uttar Pradesh and Punjab, which influence the life-styles and language of the people. Characteristics of its geographical location, its inhabitants are a race blend of tradition and intellect. They are extremely receptive to modern ideas, inventions and the fantasies of the modern social ethos. People belonging to various religious sects, castes and lingual groups live marvelously with each other, with their socio-economic status taking a back seat. Migrations from various parts of India has led to diverse culture coming together in various parts of Delhi. Durga Puja in Delhi celebrated with same enthusiasm as Id is celebrated. The Guru Purab and Christmas carry the same colour as Dewali or Buddha Purnima. The amalgamation of various cultures, traditions, religions has painted Delhi in colour which are brought from all over India.

Today Delhi is a crowded and extremely polluted modern city, which has ancient, crumbling structures cropping up unexpectedly in every area. Although sixty per cent of Delhiites are born elsewhere, the city's population has grown over twenty percent in the last decade and now stands at around 16.7 million. Rapid growth has seen Delhi spilling into the surrounding states, creating satellite developments such as Gurugram to the south. The city has been attracting its fare share of industrial development in the last two decades, with an influx of technocrats, specialists and fortune seekers to match. In a heady atmosphere of optimism, around 9000 new industrial units sprang up every year during the 1990s. Despite this new-found affluence, a staggering third of the city's population lives in the notorious jhuggies-slums often seen clinging to the edge of new developments. With a daily average of around 350 major incidents of crime, including mindless cases of murder accompanying simple robberies, Delhi has gained the dubious reputation of being the crime capital of the country. The poor aren't the only perpetrators of crime—the city's nouveau riche young, burdened with more money than sense, have been responsible for some of the most notorious recent cases.

Today, very few city residents can lay claim to being 'real' Delhi-wallahs, and most of the population of New Delhi comprises Hindu-Punjabi families originally from Lahore. In the past decade its population has increased by 20%, largely due to rapid economic expansion and increased job opportunities. The downside of this boom is increased overcrowding, traffic congestion, housing shortages and pollution.

■ DELHI FESTIVALS ■

There is perhaps not a single day in the Indian calendar when in some part of the vast country a festival is not celebrated or a fair held-replete with rituals, colour, music, feasting, pageantry, fun and frolic. Many of the festivals are subject to the lunar calendar. The Islamic festivals are celebrated according to the Muslim or the Hijri calendar. Therefore, the times the festivals are held can change from one year to the next. Delhi, being a metropolitan city, is a melting pot of cultures, traditions and festivals of the country. A whirling dervish of people, culture and religion, Delhi offers a feast of festivals for every imaginable taste. This city celebrates harvests, seasons and celestial mangoes, worships holy books and sacred stories, burns the devil and pays homage to light, and throws birthday parties for the founders of Islam, Hinduism, Jainism, Hare Krishna, Sikhism-and India. In fact, all major Indian festivals are celebrated here by different communities. The seat of empire for centuries, royal patronage ensured that Delhi remained the cultural epicentre of the country, attracting the best of painters, musicians and dancers. Delhi Tourism puts on display this rich and diverse cultural heritage by holding a series of festivals during the year. The scattered citadels of erstwhile dynasties which co-exist with high rise residential localities and crowded commercial complexes, form the picturesque backdrop for the haunting melodies and graceful dances rendered by leading artists during the festivals organised by Delhi Tourism, amongst which some of the popular ones are the Roshanara and Shalimar Bagh Festivals. These festivals mirror the multiplicity of cultures and reflect the fusion of regional diversities which constitutes modern blend most harmoniously into a whole.

Religious celebrations are a large part of Delhi's multicultural social life, and it's worth trying to take time out to enjoy the city's fanfare traditional dances and vibrant costumes. The city is a host to several secular festivals, when performers gather for music, dance and drama events.

Lohri (January): The climax of winter is celebrated with bonafires and singing in this Lohri festivities. Traditionally, Lohri marks the end of winter.

Republic Day (January): Republic Day falls on 26th January. It is the most colourful of the city's festivals events and also the biggest crowd-puller. Hundreds of thousands people line the route from Rajpath to the Red Fort to watch the pageant of soldiers, camel crops, armored regiments, brass bands, folk dancers, school children, war veterans and elaborate floats representing the cultural diversity of India. The two hour long parade is usually rounded off with a much-awaited spectacular fly-passed presented by Air Force squadrons. A special display of folk dances also takes place at the **Talkatora Stadium.**

Retreat (January): On 29th January, the departure of the British is marked by a colourful ceremony with marching bands from the armed forces, set against the imposing backdrop of the Rashtrapati Bhawan, the secretariats and the setting sun. A rehearsal is generally held on 28th January, for which tickets are also available.

Id-ul-Fitar: Id-ul-Fitar is celebrated to mark the end of Ramadaan, the Muslim month of fasting. It is an occasion for feasting and rejoicing.

Martyrs' Day (January): Martyrs' Day on 30 Jan. commemorates Mahatma Gandhi's and others' efforts for India's independence. Participants gather at Raj Ghat for prayers and music.

Sikh Festival (January): Sikh Festival is the birthday of Guru Gobind Singh Ji and is celebrated throughout the city.

Kite-Flying Festival (January): The colourful kites cascade the horizons of Delhi on Makar Sankranti, from the green lawns of Palika Bazaar,

Connaught Place, this extravaganza attracts national as well as international participants.

Basant Panchami (January-February): The biting winter winds during the end of January-early February, brings along the Hindu festival of Basant Panchami as welcome to the spring. This is the season when the prestigious Mughal garden behind Rashtrapati Bhavan are opened to public for a month.

Thyagaraja Festival (February): An enthusiastic display of south Indian music and dance, is held opposite Jawaharlal Nehru University in Vaikunthnath temple.

Garden Tourism Festival (February): Delhi is one of the greenest capitals in the world, with a long tradition of laying out of gardens, which dot the city. It is this tradition that Delhi Tourism keeps alive by holding the **Garden Tourism Festival** at the Talkatora Garden in February which is generally spread over three days and generates much enthusiasm amongst the gardening fraternity. This is not only a visual feast since Delhi is ablaze with flowers at this, but also a useful meeting ground for gardening enthusiasts, as well as fun and frolic for children of all ages because it is based on particular themes. Highlights include an on-the-spot painting competition for children, varieties of flower arrangements, cultural programmes, stalls of rare plants, amusement park, puppet/magic shows, tourism pavilions of different states of India and martial arts display. In addition, craftsmen from various parts of the country display and sell their products here.

Suraj Kund Mela (February): Suraj Kund Mela is the popular Crafts Fair held at Suraj Kund that is set in a rural ambience, with folk dancing, music and food from the different states.

Delhi Flower Show (February): Delhi Flower Show is an international horticultural exhibition of flowers, including hybrids is held on the grounds of the Purana Quila.

Holi (March): Holi, the festivals of colors, marks the onset of spring. On the eve of this exuberant Hindu spring festival, bonfires burn all over the city, symbolizing the destruction of the devil Holika. The next day, in celebration of the arrival of spring, people pelt one another with coloured paint.

Maha Shivratri (March): Maha Shivratri is celebrated on the 'Amavasya' night of 'Phalguna'. It is said, that on this dark night Lord Shiva danced the 'Tandava Nritya', (cosmic dance). He is worshipped at temples with all night vigils and prayers and unmarried women keep day-long fasts so that Shiva may grant them good husbands.

Shankarlal Sangeet Sammelan (March): Shankarlal Sangeet Sammelan, a festival of Indian music. Shriram Bharatiya Kala Kendra, 1 Copernicus Marg.

Muharram (March): Muharram is an Islamic New Year Festival that commemorates the martyrdom of Muhammad's grandson, Imam Husain.

Amir Khusrau's Anniversary (April): Amir Khusrau's anniversary is celebrated in April, with a fair in Nizamuddin, prayers and 'qawwali' singing. The event also observed as the National Festival, staged mostly at the Rabindra Bhawan.

Baisakhi (April): At the onset of summer, when the sun gets fierce in the mid of April, north India, celebrates the Hindu New Year as Baisakhi. This is also the beginning of the harvesting season.

Buddha Jayanti (May): The first full moon night in May *i.e.*, the month of Vaisakha is celebrated as Buddha Purnima, not just to commemorates Lord Buddha's birth, but also his 'Enlightenment' and gaining 'Nirvana'..... Prayer meetings are held at Buddha Vihar, Ring Road and Buddha Vihar, Mandir Marg.

Mahavir Jayanti (May): The birth of Lord Mahavira, who founded Jainism, is celebrated around this time of the year with prayers and processions.

Sikh Festival (June): In June, martyrdom of Guru Arjan Dev Ji, Sikh festival, is held throughout the city.

International Mango Festival (July): To celebrate the advent of the king of fruits, Delhi Tourism hold the Mango Festival in the month of July. Mentioned in the Vedas and Upanishads, the mango is considered auspicious and a symbol of life and joy forever. The largest producer of mangoes, India grows more than eleven hundred varieties of mangoes in different parts of the country. The Mango Festival is the place to discover the magic of mangoes in all their immense variety. Often the Talkatora stadium is a host to this peculiar event, where over five hundred different types of mango are on show, Tourists can enjoy the taste for free and view a cultural programmes. It draws people from the country as well as businessmen, both from home and abroad.

Independence Day (August): 15 August is celebrated in the city as Independence Day to mark the Indian independence from the British rule in the year 1947. The Prime minister of the nation addresses the nation from the Red Fort and many people gather to hear the Prime Minister's address.

Janmashtami (August): In August, the festival Janmashtami, celebrates the birth of Lord Krishna.

Gandhi Jayanti (October): On 2nd October, this solemn celebration honours of the birthday of Mahatma Gandhi at Raj Ghat, the site of his cremation.

Phoolwalon-ki-Sair (October): In early October, a festival specific to Mahrauli, in Delhi, takes place. This is the Phulwalon-ki-Sair or the Flower Sellers Procession, which originated in the 16th century. The highlight is a procession of people carrying decorated floral fans, which are blessed at the shrine of the 13th century Sufi saint, Khwaja Qutb-ud-din Bakhtyar Kaki and at the Hindu temple of Jogmaya, both in Mehrauli. The procession ends with a formal ceremony at the Jahaz Mahal, a 16th century pleasure resort by the side of a lake.

Qutub Festival (October): Musicians and dancers perform at night by the city's 12th century landmark, the Qutub Minar which is the venue for the Qutub Festival held in October. This festival organized by the Delhi Tourism provides tourists a glimpse of the cultural grandeur of India. Here, cultural events are held where veterans of Indian classical music and dance and folk musicians give spectacular performances.

Dussehra (October-November): Also in October is Dussehra, commemorating the victory of Lord Rama over the demon king,

Ravana. A month-long Ram Lila dance festival is organized by the Bhartiya Kala Kendra, depicting scenes from the epic Ramayana, similar presentations of the Ramayana are organized in different parts of the city. It concludes with the burning of giant effigies of Ravana, his brother Kumbhakaran and his son Meghnad.

Navratri (October-November): Navratri is a Hindu festival, that is celebrated throughout the city.

Guru Nanak Jayanti (November): The birth anniversary of Guru Nanak, the founder of Sikhism, is celebrated with great devotion.

Martyrdom of Guru (November): Martyrdom of Guru Tegh Bahadur Ji celebrated in November throughout the city.

The International Trade Fair (November): The International Trade Fair starts on the 14th of November every year. Held at the Pragati Maidan, it is a major event for the business community. Corporate houses from all over the world show their wares and business deals are finalised in a big way. The fair is also a major tourist attraction and is popular with many. Pragati Maidan is also host to many other fairs that include the Auto Expo and the Leather Fair. Throughout the year Pragati Maidan is the venue for fairs and exhibitions. The Shakuntalam theatre is located in Pragati Maidan and regular film shows are held here.

Diwali (October-November): This important Hindu festival celebrates the victory of good over evil as depicted in the epic Ramayana in the homecoming of Lord Rama after defeating Ravana. In the evening, public buildings and homes are lit up with candles or oil lamps. Fireworks add noise and colour to this festival of lights. The festival of lights is preceded by several Diwali Melas, where food, handicrafts and a variety of earthern lamps and candles are sold.

Guru Purab (November-December): Guru Purab is the celebration of the birth of first of the ten Sikh gurus, Guru Nanak. 'Nagar Kirtans' are taken out through the streets and in the Gurdwaras, 'Granthees' recite verses from the Guru Granth Sahib, the holy book of Sikhs.

Indian Dance Festivals (December): In December, the India International Centre hosts frequent performances of classical Indian dance and music. 40 Max Mueller Marg, Lodi Estate. Another dance venue is at the Hauz Khas Village, 10km south of Connaught Place. The Trevani Theatre Complex is a popular venue for year-round student and professional dance and theatre performances. 205 Tansen Marg, between Bengali Market and India Gate.

Christmas (December): On 25th of December the birth of Jesus Christ is celebrated in India, with the traditional exchange of greetings and gifts. All major hotels and restaurants in the capital host special Christmas eve entertainments, while the midnight mass and other services are organized by the churches.

New Year's Eve (December): The culmination of the Indian festive spirit is celebrated on the 31st of December, with most hotels and restaurants offering special food and entertainment packages.

Festivals in Addition: In addition, Dilli Hatt offers tantalising flimpses of the vast storehouse of Indian culture by holding regional festivals at its open air theatre. These are held from time to time throughout the year. These festivals reflect the immerse diversity, the colour and the vibrancy of this ancient land, ranging as they do from the Pongal and the Onam festivals from South India.

❐ ❐ ❐

18 Social Security

IN order to have more inclusive growth and development with a human face, Government of Delhi is giving more emphasis on (i) streamlining the delivery mechanism of the existing schemes and programmes (ii) increasing the spectrum of target groups (iii) reorienting the focus of some schemes/activities and (iv) evolving and adopting need felt programmes. Government of Delhi is thus making concerted efforts to ensure that the weaker sections of the society, disadvantaged groups and physically challenged persons get better care and support on one hand and on the other, through another batch of schemes and programmes, the Government would continue to march ahead towards economic empowerment of women and providing social security to the aged and other vulnerable groups and creating an enabling environment for children so that child right is not violated and the child have a healthy atmosphere to grow and stand on its own. The involvement and participation of civil society in general and

LADLI SCHEME

It is a new scheme introduced w.e.f. 01.01.08. Its main objective are to promote socio-economic development of the girl child by providing education-linked financial assistance. Eligibility conditions are that the girls child should be born in Delhi. Her parents must be resident of Delhi for at least 3 years prior of filling the application and the annual family income should not exceed Rs.1.00 lac per annum. The amount of financial assistance at different stages is as under :- Under this scheme Rs. 11000/- are deposited in the name of the girl child if she is born in a hospital/Nursing Home in NCT of Delhi on or after 1/1//2008 and Rs. 10000/- are deposited in the name of the girl child if she is born on or after 1/1/2008 other than the hospital. Rs. 5000/- is also deposited in the name of the girl child on admission in classes 1, VI, IX, and passing X and on admission in Class XII. The maturity amount can be claimed when the girl child attains 18 years of age and passes class-X as a regular student or takes admission in class-XII.

voluntary organizations in particular will be the cornerstone for such empowerment of the target groups. It is felt that with this approach, Government would be able to address the social concerns that come to the fore in Delhi viz. notion of well being, protection of human rights and adoption of social security measures.

Keeping the above objectives in view and also looking to the needs of giving more focused attention towards women and children, Government of Delhi in November, 2007 decided to have a separate department for Women and Child Development (WCD). The Social Welfare Department [SWD] deals with matters regarding senior citizens and Physically challenged persons and other vulnerable groups of our society, with undivided attention.

BHAGIDARI

In order to involve the people of Delhi in its governance, the Government of Delhi introduced the concept of Bhagidari, which means partnership or co-sharing. A process of dialogue and discovery of joint solutions was started with resident welfare associations, market and trader associations, civic service agencies, public utility services and various public service agencies like DVB, DJB, DDA, Delhi Police, MCD, NDMC etc. The objective was to ensure that the citizens are able deliberate and discuss their problems with officials. Another objective was to make the problem understood and devise (and implement) its workable solution like polio eradication, literacy, environment improvement etc. The first phase of the scheme was, implemented from January, 2000 to June, 2001 and it provided very useful experience. Now, the concept of partnership is being further widened and will show better results.

❐ ❐ ❐

19 Social Welfare

THROUGH a host of programmes, Government of Delhi on one hand is making concerted efforts to ensure that the weaker sections of the society, disadvantaged groups and physically challenged persons get better care and support and on the other hand through another batch of schemes and programmes, the Government is marching ahead towards providing social security to aged and other vulnerable groups. For undertaking all such welfare measures, the Social Welfare Department is the nodal department, for which they have at their disposal a network of residential care homes and non-institutional services spread all over Delhi. Details of programmes implemented by the Department are given below:

■ SCHEMES AND PROGRAMMES ■

WELFARE OF SENIOR CITIZENS

Government of Delhi has brought out "a policy for senior citizens" which is in consonance with the National Policy, at the same time addresses the specific concerns of senior citizens in NCT of Delhi. The policy considers persons of 60 years and more in age as "Senior Citizens". The policy envisages ensuring welfare of Senior Citizens and improving quality of their lives. It aims at providing assistance to enable them to cope with the problems of old age. It also proposes affirmative action by the Government Departments in collaboration with civil society for ensuring that the existing public services for Senior Citizens are made more user friendly and sensitive to the needs of Senior Citizens. Government of Delhi would also consider to have a public education mechanism to prepare people for old age persons in order to ensure that they are able to grow gracefully and remain financially secure in their later years.

There are a number of schemes being implemented by Social Welfare Department for Welfare of Senior Citizens.

PENSION TO SENIOR CITIZEN

This scheme is being implemented by Department of Social Welfare. Under this scheme, pension is remitted on quarterly basis in the saving accounts of the beneficiaries maintained in the bank, through Electronic Clearing System (ECS) of RBI. The persons resident of Delhi for five years with proof, age of 60 years and above and having family income less than ₹ 60,000/- per annum are eligible. The income does not include income of independent sons and daughters. The recommendation of area MLA/MP/Gazetted Officer of State/Central Government is necessary. The applicant must have a valid ID proof as listed in notification. From April 2008, rate of pension was enhanced from ₹ 600/- pm to ₹ 1000/- per month. The Quantum of financial assistance to senior citizens of 70 years and above has been enhanced from ₹ 1000/- to ₹ 1500/- per month w.e.f. October, 2011.

OLD AGE HOMES

The aim and objective of the plan scheme 'Setting up of Old Age Homes' is to provide a place to senior citizens where they may live gracefully in a congenial atmosphere. Under the scheme residential care including free boarding and lodging facilities, health care, reading room, recreation facilities, common prayer place and discourses etc. are being provided. Presently two homes are functioning at Lampur and Bindapur. Due to the renovation work the inmates of Tilak Vihar old age home have been shifted to Bindapur old age home.

The Department of Women and Child Development is implementing the plan scheme 'Pension to Women in Distress' i.e., widowed, divorced, separated and destitute women by way of providing financial assistance. The Plan Scheme was introduced in year 2007-08 to help economically poor widows with regular source of income in term of monthly pension of ₹ 600/- per month in the age group of 18 years to below 60 years whose family income was up to ₹ 48000/- per annum and resident of Delhi for more than five years. From April 2008, the family income ceiling has been enhanced to ₹ 60000/- per annum and also amount of financial assistance was enhanced to ₹ 1000/- per month.

Under the plan scheme 'Financial Assistance to Widow for Performing Marriage of their daughter/orphan Girls', an amount of ₹ 25,000/- was given in 2011-12. The amount of financial assistance has been enhanced from ₹ 25,000/- to ₹ 30,000/- from April 2012. The beneficiary must be a bonafide resident of Delhi. The benefit is given only up to 2 girls in the family. The Family income ceiling was enhanced from ₹ 48,000/- to ₹ 60,000/- per annum since April 2008.

DELHI FAMILY BENEFIT SCHEME

The objective of the scheme is to provide assistance to poor households on the events of the death of the breadwinner. Amount of benefit is ₹ 20,000/- in case of death of primary breadwinner, irrespective of the cause of death viz. natural or accidental.

WELFARE OF LEPROSY AFFECTED PERSONS

A Rehabilitation Center for Leprosy [RCL] affected person was established during the year 1980-81. At present S.W. Department is paying ₹ 1800/- p.m. to RCL beneficiaries as financial assistance. The RCL is not a residential home. Most of the beneficiaries are residing in different areas of Delhi such as Tahirpur [Trans Yamuna], R.K. Puram, Sri Niwas Puri and Patel Nagar etc. The major colony of Leprosy affected persons is Tahirpur where Shelter workshop and Training cum Production center are located. In these centers, department provides production work facilities to enable leprosy affected persons to stand on their own legs and to make them economically independent. In these centers, department provides training facilities in handloom weaving, shoe-making, chalk making, handloom class etc.

OTHER WELFARE MEASURES

Many poor people who suffer from TB do not get adequate attention mainly due to negligence or financial constraints, the Social Welfare Department provides financial assistance @ ₹ 300/- per month to each TB patient for their treatment.

MISSION CONVERGENCE (SAMAJIK SUVIDHA SANGAM)

Mission Convergence is an initiative to address the issues of socio-economic vulnerability of marginalized and excluded communities in Delhi. The mission has developed a new Vulnerability based criteria for identifying beneficiaries for welfare schemes. At the grass root level, NGOs have been partnered for setting up Gender Resource Centre-Suvidha Kendra's (GRC-SKs), which will act as outreach centers in the community and serve as the first point of contact for the citizens.

❑ ❑ ❑

Miscellaneous 20

DELHI HIGH COURT

The High Court of Delhi was established on 31st October 1966. Initially, the High Court of Delhi exercised jurisdiction not only over the Union Territory of Delhi, but also Himachal Pradesh. It had a Himachal Pradesh Bench at Shimla in a building called Ravenswood. The High Court of Delhi continued to exercise 

jurisdiction over Himachal Pradesh until the State of Himachal Pradesh Act, 1970 was enforced on 25th January 1971.

The sanctioned strength of Judges of this High Court increased from time to time. Presently, the sanctioned strength of Judges of the High Court of Delhi is 45 permanent Judges and 15 Additional Judges.

HEALTH

Delhi has one of the best health infrastructures in India both qualitatively and quantitatively. Delhi offers among the most sophisticated medical care with the latest State-of-the-art technology for treatment and the best-qualified doctors in the country. Delhi has some of the finest Super Speciality Hospitals of India. Due to their expertise and repute, these hospitals are attracting patients from all over the world. It is estimated that about one third of patient in major hospitals of Delhi come from the neighboring states. Government agencies such as MCD, NDMC, Railways, Cantonment Board, ESI, Central Government besides Delhi Government's own network of dispensaries and hospitals are instrumental in delivery of health care services to Delhities.

Delhi's health network has enabled the city to achieve key demographic/health indices.

POVERTY LINE

The Planning Commission estimates the proportion and number of poor separately for rural and urban India at the National and State levels based in the recommendations of the Task Force on 'Projections of Minimum Needs and Effective Consumption Demands' (1979). The Task Force had defined the poverty line (BPL) as the cost of an all India average consumption basket at which calorie norms were met. The norms were 2400 calories per capita per day for rural areas and 2100 calories for urban areas. These calorie norms have been expressed in monetary terms as Rs. 49.09 and Rs. 56.64 per capita per month for rural and urban areas respectively at 1973-74 prices. Based on the recommendations of a Study Group on 'The Concept and Estimation of Poverty Line', the private consumption deflator from national accounts statistics was selected to update the poverty lines in 1977-78, 1983 and 1987-88.

Subsequently, the expert group under the Chairmanship of late Prof. D.T. Lakdawala examined the issue. The Expert Group accepted the definition of poverty line and base year figures but suggested an alternative methodology to calculate the poverty line. It recommended the use of consumer price index for agricultural labour to update the rural poverty line and a simple average of weighted commodity indices of the consumer price index for industrial workers and for urban non-manual employees to update the urban poverty line. The Planning Commission accepted the recommendations of the Expert Group but modified the method for updating the poverty lines. The Commission decided to use only CPI for industrial workers to estimate and update the urban poverty line. The estimates have been revised and released accordingly.

The Planning commission released State Specific Poverty Line and their number on the basis of NSS 61st round (July 2004 – June 2005). Accordingly, the poverty line for rural Delhi was estimated as ₹ 410.38 as against All India estimates for same sector at ₹ 356.30. Like-wise in case of urban Delhi, the poverty line has worked out to ₹ 612.91 as against ₹ 538.60 at the All India level. The total number of people below poverty line in Delhi comes to 22.93 lakhs which amount to 14.7% of the total population. Sector-wise break-up revealed that 6.9% of the rural population (0.63 lakhs) and 15.2% of the urban population (22.30 lakhs) were estimated to be below poverty line. The number of people below poverty line have nearly doubled in Delhi, i.e., 11.49 lakhs in 1999-2000 to 22.93 lakhs during 2004-2005 which is a matter of concern.

IMPORTANT NEWSPAPERS AND MAGAZINES

English Dailies: *The Hindustan Times, The Times of India, The Indian Express, The Statesman, The Hindu, The Pioneer, The National Herald, The Asian Age, The Economic Times*

Hindi Dailies: *Dainik Bhaskar, Nav Bharat Times, Hindustan, Jansatta, Rashtriya Sahara, Dainik Jagran, Punjab Kesri, Veer Arjun, Sandhya Times.*

Urdu Dailies: *Qaumi Awaz, Awam, Pratap, Milap*

Magazines: *India Today, Outlook, Mayapuri, Nai Duniya, Vikas Setu, Rashtriya Sahara, Alive, Indian Observer, Sarita, Competition Success Review, Civil Services Chronicle, News and Events, Women's Era, Crime and Detective, Ajkal, Griha Shobha, Filmi Duniya, Filmi Kaliyan, Sushma, Madhur Kathayen, Nandan, Shama, Punjabi Digest*

News Agencies: Some of the leading news and feature agencies like the Press Trust of India (PTI), United News of India (UNI), Varta, Bhasha, India Press Agency and Indian News and Feature Alliance are located in Delhi. Similarly, some of the important foreign news agencies like Reuters, Tass (Russia), Associated Press, United Press International (USA) and Jiji Press (Japan) also function from Delhi. Almost every foreign embassy or mission brings out its own publications.

ELECTRONIC MEDIA

Radio: Delhi was the first among those cities where radio stations were set up by the Government of India after it took over the broadcasting services in the country. Established in 1935 with two medium power transmitters (one of medium-wave frequency transmitter and the other one of short wave freequency) and temporary studios located at Alipur road, it went on the air on January 1, 1936. During the Second World War, the programme activities at Delhi Station of the All India Radio increased both in terms of volume and variety. A high power transmitting centre was established at Delhi along with a number of high power and medium power shortwave transmitters. The construction of the new broadcasting house in New Delhi was completed in 1943 incorporating the latest advances in the techniques of studio design. Today, Delhi has a number of transmitters of varying strengths, which with suitable combinations, broadcast offered by the radio station. A new high power transmission centre has been set up near Khampur. The service on the medium wave frequency is now available on four different channels, including the popular Vividh Bharati Service. A new youth service was also introduced for the first time in the country from the Delhi station in 1969. Besides catering to the needs of Delhi and its neighbouring states, the Delhi station of All India Radio functions as the national station of AIR. Programmes designed for all-India listening mostly originate from Delhi. Such programmes are broadcast over a number of wave transmitters in order to enable regional stations of AIR to pick up these broadcasts and relay them to their own regional transmitters. The main news bulletins in various languages, national programmes of talks, music, plays, features, broadcasts to the nation by high dignitaries and special programmes arranged on important national days or anniversaries are among such broadcasts as emanate from the Delhi station but are made available to other stations of AIR for broadcasting. AIR is also operating two FM station in Delhi.

Television: On August 15, 1959, television was introduced for the first time in the country as a pilot scheme, operating from All India Radio's television centre in Delhi. The experimental television service was converted into a regular service from January 1, 1962. The duration of the service gradually increased with the expansion of studio facilities. The television service at present is available at the national level. Doordarshan has an extensive network to serve the broad objective of information, education and entertainment. In September, 1984, the first multi-channel transmission was introduced in Delhi, offering viewers many choices in news, entertainment and channel variety. There are now several low power/high power transmitters linked with Delhi through INSATs for the telecast of the national programme. Private satellite T.V. channels have also entered the fray. These compete with one another for viewers' attention and introduce mesmerising programmes. Most of the news and current affairs channels are based in Delhi as it is a centre of national political and economic activity and important decisions are taken at the central level.

❏ ❏ ❏

1908